The Diary

Rachel Bauer

THE COMPLETE SERIES

A Lines From Lancaster County Saga

*"Teach me thy way, O LORD,
and lead me in a plain path"*

Psalm 27:11

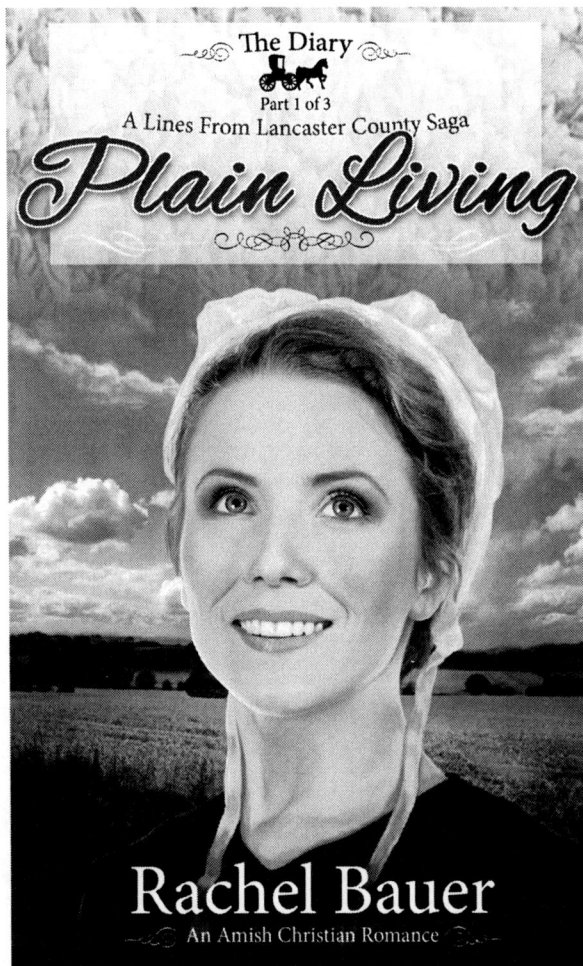

The Diary

Part 1 of 3

A Lines From Lancaster County Saga

Plain Living

Rachel Bauer

An Amish Christian Romance

Chapter One

"No sir," explained Sadie calmly. "We can not deliver your table on Sunday. My father and Abram will deliver it on Monday." Sadie closed her eyes and listened to the irritated man on the other end of the phone call. "Yes sir, the table is finished, but we do not deliver on Sundays. The terms on the website are clear, and my father told you that Monday is the earliest we can deliver it." She listened again and held the phone away from her ear as the man's volume increased. "Sir, if you want your Amish made table, it will be delivered on Monday. If you want a table on Sunday, it won't be made or delivered by Amish." Sadie paused and finished, "Then we'll see you on Monday. Thank you sir."

Samuel Zook looked at his daughter. He nodded and in his calm, deep voice acknowledged her skill. "Plain, honest, and humble. As God wills it, Sadie."

Sadie returned the nod, took a deep breath, and returned to the stack of receipts that she was putting in chronological order. She loved to hear the praise from her father, but she reminded herself that she mustn't become too proud. She had only recently taken over answering the phone at her father's shop, and the contact with Englisher strangers was still new to her. She knew she was good at it though, and certainly God had made her better suited to the job than her father's apprentice, Abram.

At twenty-one, Abram Byler should have begun to develop some of the peaceful calm that Sadie's father radiated. Instead, pious and devout, Abram had trouble keeping an even temper when dealing with the Englishers who sought out Ephrata Woodworks' beautifully handmade furniture. He frequently lost his patience and had been short and abrupt with too many customers within Samuel Zook's hearing. Choosing a daughter as the voice on the phone – the person between the shop and the outside world – was unusual among the Plain people, but Samuel made that decision as he did all of the others in his life – calmly and practically.

Sadie bent her head to continue sorting the records of last month's business, and spoke to her father. "We have more receipts for May than we did for April. I will have the May paperwork ready for Abram to take home this evening."

"Good, Sadie. I will send Abram inside before he goes home. I have your sister's chest to finish now." Samuel left the store front and headed out the back to the large workshop where he and Abram Byler labored to make the furniture whose sales supported the large Zook family and might one day support young Abram Byler's family as well.

As Samuel crossed the yard between his store and his workshop, he reflected on the peace and good fortune that God had given him. His business had grown to the point at which he could be selective about the jobs he chose. He could have built Zook Woodworks to be much larger, but to earn more than he needed to keep his family safe, fed, and comfortable would have been prideful. His satisfaction in his work was that he could live the life God intended and that he fashioned beautiful things using the talent God had given him.

"Sadie will have the business receipts for you to take to your father this evening. And the Schneider table will be delivered on Monday as promised."

Abram bristled, "Did Mr. Schneider give Sadie trouble? Those Englishers always want things their own way. They want to boast of their Amish made table to their proud friends, and they never…"

"Abram, we have work to do," Samuel calmly interrupted. "God has given us work to occupy our bodies so that we need not worry our minds. Plain living keeps us humble and separate. We need not trouble ourselves with Englisher ways."

Chastened, Abram nodded at Samuel. "Will we finish Esther's chest today?"

"Ja, she will want to have it when Miriam is married. If God wills it, there will be a marriage to celebrate in November. Samuel expected that his eldest daughter, Miriam, would be married this year after the harvest was complete. She had been going for drives with Luke Stoltzfus, and they seemed to be of like mind on the matter. As Samuel began to prepare the stain for his youngest daughter's hope chest, he thought on how God had found a good man to marry his Miriam. Luke was steady, modest, and a hard worker in his father's dairy. He would be a good husband. He hoped for men as good for little Esther, only seven years old, and Sadie, at nineteen.

Back in the storefront, Sadie quickly and neatly sorted the remaining May receipts and, with a glance at the window to check for her father or Abram's approach, slid a slim notebook from between the files neatly organized behind the counter. As she opened the notebook, she reached for the pen she kept tucked behind her right ear, the pen's end secured underneath her black bonnet. As she started a fresh page with the current date, she wondered again what her father would say if he caught her writing in her journal.

Sadie worried a lot about her secret writing. She wondered if God would think her proud for taking time from her work for something so personal, an activity that had no value to her family. After all, it's not as though her brothers and sisters would eat her journal, and it's not as though her scribbling could be sold like the beautiful furniture that her father and Abram made.

It always came down to the same thing though. Why would God have made her want to write if it were wrong? She didn't boast of her writing – but then how could she when it was a secret? She knew that her little stories about her life were fair and true depictions of her life in rural Ephrata, Pennsylvania. She knew that she didn't write of anything unseemly, and she knew that she loved to write. God made her to love to write. And write she would.

The journal she kept hidden at her father's shop was filled with some of her experiences with Englishers. Though she found outsiders difficult at times, unwilling to understand the values of the craftsmen who made such desirable furniture, she tried to deal with them humbly and patiently. She also recorded some of these interactions. She was scrupulously honest, and had quite a talent for recording their words, attitudes, and peculiarities, especially given that she'd had so little contact with people other than Plain folk for most of her nineteen years.

The man from Philadelphia wanted his table delivered on Sunday before his boss came over for dinner. He didn't understand that we don't work on Sundays. I don't understand how you could be so proud to boast of Amish workmanship without respect for our day of worship. God gives us these lessons to show us why we must keep ourselves apart from the world.

Da is happy with the way I talked to the Englisher. He feels better now that Abram doesn't answer the phone and make customers angry. Why does Abram get so angry at the Englishers? If he jealous of the way they live in the world?

The man and woman who came in the store yesterday tried to be so polite, but they talked so loud and so slow, as if they didn't expect me to understand English very well. When they walked in, my father and I were speaking in Pennsylvania German, as we always do when we are with our people. They listened and looked at us like we were from another world.

The woman in her high heels and short skirt talked to me like I was a baby. She asked about the prices of our hope chests. She wanted one for her office to make it look less formal and more rustic. She also wanted to go directly to the craftsmen so that she could tell the tale of meeting the people whose hands created such lovely work. I got the feeling that she thought our family could use the money as well. She thought she would offer help to people who had to live so plainly. It almost felt like she was offering charity rather than paying a fair price for Da's hard work. I think she felt sorry for us, and I guess that if you are proud to live in a busy place and drive a fancy car, that the way we live might seem pitiful in comparison.

I smiled at her and answered her questions. Da tells me that we should take every chance we have to show that being honest, plain, and humble is the best way to live. As the lady and I talked, she began to look at me differently – like I was a person rather than a peculiar circus attraction. She picked out the chest that she wanted, and asked if our shop accepted checks or just cash. I told her, of course, that we accepted cash or credit cards, and she looked at me with disbelief.

She didn't think that the Amish would use credit card machines or any kind of electricity at all. I pointed at the light fixtures that lit the room. I pointed at the air conditioning vents that would cool the room this summer. I showed her our credit card machine, and I explained that we have a gas-powered generator that supplies the power that we need to do business. She seemed almost disappointed – as if her "authentic Amish" experience were tarnished by this intrusion of her modern world. But by the time she and her husband left the store, I think she understood more about Plain living than she did when she walked in.

As I walked across the yard to get Abram to help her husband load the chest into their enormous truck, I thought about how every encounter I had with the English was a chance to show that being Plain isn't pitiful. It seems to me that there is value in demonstrating our humility and honesty and that perhaps the English can learn that there is more to life than just fancy cars and material things they don't need. Of course, it's nice that they buy our furniture.

Sadie finished her entry, closed the journal, and was about to replace it in the gap between her files that she regularly used to conceal her writing when the phone rang. Sadie jumped a little, as she was still not used to the shrill interruption of her usually peaceful routine, and since they didn't have a telephone at home, the sound was startling. "Ephrata Woodworks," she declared, as she answered the phone. "How may I help you?"

The rest of Sadie's day passed at a steadily busy pace. She fielded a few more phone calls, discussed her father's workmanship with a couple who stopped in to window shop, and she boxed up the sales receipts as well as the monthly expenses for Abram to take home to his father, John, the accountant for many of the successful Amish businesses in Ephrata.

"Samuel told me you have monthly work to go to my father," Abram explained as he stuck his head in the door of the storefront. Dusty and hot after a long day in the workshop, Abram was reluctant to disturb Sadie's quiet, neat workspace. He felt out of place in her shop that smelled of furniture polish and the sweet cinnamon smell that always accompanied Sadie.

Sadie nodded at Abram and waved him inside the store. As he ducked his head to enter, Sadie stood behind the counter, smoothed her dark blue dress, and tucked her pen behind her ear. "I have the work for your father here," she told Abram as she stacked the last of the files for John Byler into the box before she closed it up. "I had to find a bigger box. We have more receipts than we did in April," Sadie explained.

As Abram crossed the room to get the paperwork, Sadie studied him with her placid, even gaze. He was tall, even taller than her father, and his neat brown hair was covered in a fine layer of sawdust. He smelled like hard work and fresh cut wood, and his clean-shaven jawline was an unnecessary reminder to Sadie that he was unmarried.

"I'll let him know that God has blessed you again this month," Abram said, as he collected the box from Sadie. "And as it's God's blessings that give you success, you should not be too proud, Sadie Zook, "Abram proclaimed. As he said the words, he wished he could take them back. What was it that made him sound so pompous every time he talked to Sadie? Though he was only two years older than she, everything he said came out all wrong – as if he were trying to sound like a grown man, married and secure.

Sadie looked directly at Abram, her calm gaze never wavering, and replied, "Abram, I thank you for the reminder." She turned her back on Abram and hid her smile behind the edge of her bonnet. Abram always seemed so formal, so awkward when he spoke to her alone. And a shame, too, Sadie thought, as such a hard worker and such a good man would make some girl a good husband. Sadie had long ago given up any chance of catching the eye of Abram Byler. Clearly, she thought, he had no interest or thought for her other than his desire to correct her imagined flaws.

"Good night to you, "Abram hurriedly replied, as he easily shifted the box to one hip and opened the door to escape outside. Carefully placing the box in the cargo space of his open courting buggy, Abram sighed as he rested his forehead against the smooth fiberglass of his most cherished possession. "Why do I always act like such a fool?" Abram whispered to himself. "You would think I'd never spoken to a girl before in my life."

Hitching his horse to his buggy, Abram reflected on his difficulty in having a normal conversation with Sadie. She was the only girl he had trouble talking to. He'd driven many eager young women home from church on Sunday evenings, and he had no trouble finding things to talk about with other girls. Sadie somehow left him uncomfortably tongue-tied, though. Since he couldn't find anything normal to say, Abram found himself resorting to the only thing that came to mind, which was inevitably a criticism. Sadie most likely thought him insufferable.

As Abram began his two-mile journey home, he thought more about Sadie Zook. She was different from the other girls he knew. She dressed just the same, neat and modest and plain. She wore her hair just as other girls did, twisted up and hidden away under her sheer white prayer cap and black bonnet, a bonnet she would trade when she married for the white bonnet worn by married women. Why did thinking about Sadie always make him think about marriage, Abram wondered. She probably didn't even like him since he always seemed to be such an awkward fool around her. Abram tried to console himself by the thought that Sadie Zook was really an ordinary girl, and nothing particularly special. He almost believed it.

As Abram made his way home from the woodworking shop, Sadie, tidied up the storefront and waited for her father to finish work and fetch her for their drive home. She neatened up the stacks of custom order forms, rounded up pens and pencils to put them in the drawer where they belonged, and with a few moments to spare, Sadie decided to write a few more lines in her journal. She reached for the book in its usual spot, slipped between the vertical files for the jobs in production in the shop and the files for jobs completed awaiting delivery.

Sadie froze. The journal wasn't in its place. Thinking that she must have carelessly misplaced it, Sadie moved in a frenzy, far different from her usual competent, calm demeanor. She rapidly shuffled though the files and folders. She checked the drawers and cabinets that held office supplies. She stood behind her counter – a counter in which everything had a place and order was carefully maintained, and she felt her panic increasing. The journal was nowhere to be found. It was gone and the only possible explanation was that she'd mistakenly placed it in the box of accounting paperwork and the journal was on its way home with Abram Byler. Sadie was terrified and realized that she couldn't possibly have placed her secret in worse hands. Pompous Abram Byler had her journal, and it was only a matter of time before he or his father discovered it.

Chapter Two

Abram leaned back from the large table and looked around at his family. His father, John, removed his glasses and rubbed his eyes before nodding at his wife, Ruth, to acknowledge the bountiful dinner the family had just enjoyed. Ruth stood, and without prompting the girls, twenty-two-year-old Sarah and eleven-year-old Katie joined her in beginning to clear the table. Abram and his brothers, eighteen-year-old Joshua and fifteen-year-old John sat for a few moments more to talk to their father before beginning the evening chores.

"I brought you the Zook's May receipts, Father," Abram announced. "The box is larger than usual because Sadie said there are more sales."

"If you'll put the papers on my desk, I will use the box to take the eggs to market tomorrow," John replied. "Let's get the chores done so we can have a little time before bed."

Abram stood, pushed his chair in, and thought about how much he still missed having his oldest brother around to help with evening chores. Joseph had married last December and Abram still missed their easy companionship as they tended the small farm before the end of each day. Joshua and John worked hard, but their chatter seemed childish compared to the sober talk of faith and marriage that Abram and Joseph had shared.

"I'll bring the papers in and take the box back outside before I start on the barn," Abram told his father. "Don't take too long to get to work, boys," Abram admonished his brothers. "We still have work to do before dark."

Abram left the dining room of his family's snug home and headed for the barn where the family's two buggies and wagons were kept. His spotless courting buggy had been lovingly wiped down before Abram had put it away. He knew pride was a sin, but Abram took great pleasure in keeping his buggy looking as new as the day he bought it nearly a year ago. He loved to use the buggy for its named purpose – taking young women home after Sunday church services. He wished he had found the right woman, though: the girl who looked and felt just right on the long, slow drives home.

Certain it was just a coincidence, Abram thought about Sadie Zook as he reached for the box of papers in the buggy's cargo space. He slid the box toward him, hoisted it from the buggy, and thought about how Sadie would look in his buggy. He wondered if he would spend the whole ride with nothing to say. Or worse yet, would he spend the whole ride sounding like a disapproving bishop? Usually confident and sure, Abram never felt so awkward as when he talked to Sadie.

Resolving to be less formal the next time they spoke, Abram thought about what he might say to Sadie the next day at the store. He pondered a way to start a conversation that would seem natural as he carried the box inside and placed it on his father's desk. He opened the box, took out the first two files, neatly marked in Sadie's even script. He stacked the "May 2013 Sales" file atop a second file with the same label. As Abram looked back in the box, he noticed a small notebook with a plain green fabric cover. He picked it up, set it aside, and reached for the files that held the records of expenses and ongoing work. He neatly stacked the folders next to the sales records and glanced down at the notebook.

He was puzzled. He'd been shuttling monthly paperwork home from the store to his father for the three years he'd worked with Samuel Zook. He was familiar with the neatly labeled files, but this notebook was clearly something new. He touched the cover, picked up the small book, and ran his finger along the edge. Wondering what might be inside, Abram opened the cover. He saw a page filled with Sadie's neat handwriting, and, not quite sure why, he glanced back at the open door to his father's office before he began to read.

Abram had only read a few words before he realized that Sadie had never intended for anyone else to see this book. Before he knew it, Abram was smiling to himself and turning the page to read the rest of the story about a man who had insisted that he wanted his Amish table to be blessed by an Amish priest. As the sound of Ruth and the girls in the kitchen interrupted Abram's concentration, he quickly slammed the little book closed, slipped it into the back of the waist of his pants. Never before had Abram even thought of how useful pockets would be in his pants, as he quickly concealed the book under his clothing.

As Abram grabbed the empty box, he asked himself what he was doing. Why had he hidden the book, and what was he going to do with it? Quickly deciding to slip upstairs before he returned to start his chores, Abram darted into the room that he had until recently shared with Joseph. Slipping the book from the waist of his pants, he laid his hand on the green cover, paused, and slid the little book under his pillow.

Before he could think twice, Abram headed back downstairs and hoped that he would manage to get outside without being questioned about his furtive behavior. Stepping onto the kitchen, Abram cleared his throat and asked "Mama, do you need more eggs if the hens have laid them?"

Ruth looked inside the refrigerator and replied, "No, Abram, we have enough for tomorrow's baking. Thank you, son." Ruth returned to her talk with her daughters, something about a new buggy for the middle Stoltzfus boy, and Abrams thoughts turned to Sadie. With a blush he didn't want to explain, Abram hurried outside to find his father.

Walking toward the barn, Abram stopped in his tracks. Had he done wrong by hiding Sadie's book? Should he march up to his father and confess his sin and the sin that he was sure Sadie had committed as well? He took a few more halting steps and stopped again. Surely Sadie was taking time away from her work to write in this silly little book. Surely the book was proof of her selfishness and pride. But what if Abram told John and John talked to Samuel or even to the bishop?

Thinking quickly, Abram decided that he would wait to make a decision. Maybe he should read a little more of the journal before he took action that could make things harder for Sadie. Picking up his pace, Abram walked into the barn, set the empty box near his father's buggy, and turned to his chores.

❀ ❀ ❀

Exactly five miles away, Sadie was not exactly herself. She usually found pleasure in the repetition of tasks day after day. She didn't mind clearing and washing dishes. She found peace in the quiet conversation with her mother and her sisters. This evening was different, though. Miriam talked happily to her mother, Hannah, about her favorite songs. The unspoken reason for the discussion was an informal selection of songs that Miriam would like to be sung at her wedding. Since there were still several months before Miriam's engagement to Luke Stoltzfus would be announced, everyone in the room pretended to be having a hypothetical discussion.

Usually, Sadie would have gaily joined in and even encouraged little Esther to gently tease Miriam about her upcoming nuptials, but her mind was exactly five miles away – in her journal that was currently beneath Abram Byler's pillow. Sadie was terrified. She hadn't written anything inappropriate, of course, but it was the fact that she had written at all that she feared would cause a problem.

What were the chances, she wondered, that Abram would find the journal? Would it be better for John to find it? Was there any chance at all that it had fallen out and had been lost forever alongside the road that Abram traveled to return home each day? Sadie knew that wishing for such luck was futile, and probably evidence of pride as well. Why hadn't she hidden to book more carefully? Why had she written it at all? Why on earth did Abram Byler have to be the one to find it?

Sadie stopped drying the large earthenware mixing bowl when she realized that her mother and sisters were staring at her. "What?" she asked. "I was thinking about a customer in the store today. I'm sorry I was somewhere else."

Miriam and Hannah picked up the conversation as if nothing had happened, but Sadie knew that she needed to clear her heart and mind of her worry and let God's will determine her fate. As the last of the dishes were dried and put away, Sadie asked to be excused to her room early rather than sitting down with the rest of the family in the sitting room. Esther would miss her help with the puzzle they'd been working on over the last few nights, but Sadie knew that she wouldn't be very good company until she had prayed about her problem.

Deliberately placing her foot on each step as she ascended to the second floor, Sadie had so much running through her mind that she had trouble making sense of her thoughts. She reached her room – the smallest in the house – and was thankful for her tiny room that afforded her the only completely private bedroom in the house. Sadie untied her apron and hung it on one of the pegs that held her entire wardrobe, and she sank down to sit on the edge of her twin bed.

As she wondered about her journal – if Abram had found it and what he might have done with it – Sadie, typically a calm, steady girl, began to worry. What if John Byler spoke to her father? How could she explain her taking the time away from her work to do something so selfish as writing? As Sadie readied herself to bed, she coaxed herself back to a calmer state and decided that if she prayed, that God would sort things out in the right way, according to His will. Sadie drifted off to sleep and tried not to think about seeing Abram at her father's shop in the morning.

❀ ❀ ❀

Abram dried his face and hands. He had done his chores properly, but he wasn't quite sure how he had managed. All he could think about was the little book that waited under his pillow. His family was still downstairs in the sitting room, each one reading, talking, or playing a game. Abram had complained of being tired and declared his intentions to go to bed early. He closed the door to his bedroom – his alone now since Joseph had gotten married. He hung his clothing on the pegs in his room and readied himself for bed. Only after he was in bed and under the covers did Abram let himself slip his hand under his pillow and feel for the book concealed there.

As Abram opened the book, he wondered again if he should read it or simply turn it over to his father. He also thought that perhaps he should return it to Sadie without having read it. Finally, telling himself that if he read a little further that he'd be able to make a more complete and moral decision, Abram continued reading where he'd left off earlier that evening. As he turned the pages, occasionally stifling a laugh to keep from drawing attention from his family downstairs, Abram realized that the book was almost completely comprised of tales about Ephrata Woodwork's Englisher customers.

As Abram closed the book, replaced it under his pillow, and turned off his light, he thought about how different he felt about Englishers when Sadie described them. Before Sadie had come to work with her father, Abram had often been needed in the store front, but he had trouble remaining calm with the casual, worldly customers who stopped, to Abram's mind, only to gawk at the Plain people. The Englishers that Sadie wrote about were much more open and more considerate than Abram had thought they could be. Sadie somehow managed to find ways to connect with the outsiders while still retaining her humility and devotion to God. Abram was puzzled.

Eyes finally closing after his long work day, Abram drifted to sleep thinking about Sadie and wondering what he would say when he saw her the next morning.

Chapter Three

The June day started for both Sadie and Abram before dawn. Sadie helped Miriam and Esther with collecting and washing clothes. Since the girls could see the stars, they knew the day would dawn clear. They hung the clean clothes neatly on the lines that stretched from the house to the barn. After the laundry was done, Sadie collected the eggs from the henhouse, chatting with each of the hens as she went. She complimented each chicken on the lovely eggs she had laid, but with every task Sadie completed, she couldn't help but think about Abram and try not to worry about what he had done with her journal. Worry was a waste of time, she told herself. God would take care of her troubles.

As she braided and twisted her long, honey colored hair into a neat bun, Sadie let her thoughts drift for a moment. Her heart raced a bit as she covered her hair with her prayer cap and bonnet and thought about seeing Abram later that morning. Realizing how silly she was, Sadie shook herself from her daydream and scolded herself for wasting her thoughts on such an unyielding and harsh man as Abram Byler.

❊ ❊ ❊

The Byler farm slowly came to life before the sun was up. Ruth and Katie started bread to rise while Sarah gathered eggs from sleepy hens and the men tended their two cows and their horses. Abram did his chores automatically, for his mind was several miles away. He'd decided that he would talk to Sadie first, before he told anyone else about her book. Abram wasn't quite sure why he sped through his work more quickly than usual.

Hitching the horse to his buggy, Abram thought about what he should say to Sadie. He wondered if she even knew that her little green book was missing. During his drive to the shop, Abram organized his thoughts. Clearly Sadie needed to stop spending her time at work scribbling in her notebook, and Abram figured that she must know it. After all, if she weren't doing anything wrong, why would she be hiding the book?

Abram rolled into the shop a little earlier than usual. Sadie and Samuel wouldn't arrive for another hour or so, and Abram got his horse situated and settled in to work. Finding that work helped quiet his mind, Abram smoothly planed the pieces of wood that were destined to become some young woman's hope chest. Abram lost himself in the calming and repetitive work, and almost before he knew it, he heard the sound of the Zook's buggy arriving at the shop.

Carefully placing the plane back on his workbench, Abram took a deep breath and brushed the wood shavings from his sleeves. He paused just before he opened the door and he felt so odd, so nervous, that he nearly turned around and went back to work. Samuel would expect him, though, and as he always unhitched the Zook's horse when they arrived, his absence would be noticed.

Opening the door and stepping out into the clear, bright sunlight, Abram greeted Sadie and Samuel with a hand shading his eyes from the glare. "Good morning to you both," Abram declared in a voice a little deeper than usual. His solemn, formal tone made Sadie smile just slightly in spite of her anxiety. "I've started work on the chest for the Englishers from Maryland," he continued, "and I will finish the rocking chair for Bishop King this afternoon." As he began to lead the horse from the buggy, Abram couldn't help but glance at Sadie. Startled to find her clear blue eyes focused right on his, he looked away, fumbled with the reins, and led the horse to a watering trough.

Sadie didn't have to wonder whether Abram had found her book. She knew he had. He didn't usually pay attention to her unless he was criticizing her behavior, so his glance had to mean that he knew her secret. As she clambered out of the buggy, Sadie decided that she would wait and let Abram make the first move. She could be patient.

Sadie reached back inside the buggy to retrieve the

basket that held the lunch she'd prepared for the three of them to share, and as she turned to walk into the store, Sadie stopped short. Abram had returned from tending to the horse, and he looked at her. He took several quick steps toward her and gently lifted the basket from Sadie's arm.

"That looks heavy," Abram gruffly muttered. "I will carry it for you."

Sadie smiled to herself as the tall young man put his arm through the handle of the basket – the same basket that she had carried inside each and every day she'd worked at her father's shop. Sadie led the way across the yard and unlocked the door to the store.

"Why thank you, Abram," she said pleasantly. Wondering if Abram's strict and bossy manner might have unexpectedly softened, Sadie extended her hand to take the basket. "I appreciate the help."

"I…I…," Abram hesitated. "You look tired," he blurted. Eyes widening at how silly he sounded, Abram tried to recover. "I mean, the basket looked heavy," he spit out. "Well, and I…I…want," Abram said, and then he hesitated. The words began to spill from his lips like a torrent. "I want to talk to you. I have to talk to you. You have to talk to me," Abram blurted.

Eyes wide, Sadie calmly regarded Abram. As she opened her mouth to reply, she and Abram jumped as the shrill ring of the telephone interrupted them. Abram started, as if he'd been jolted awake, turned, and darted out the door. Sadie stood, open-mouthed, and watched him leave the building. "Ephrata Woodworks," she answered automatically as she shook her head, puzzled by Abram's actions.

Sadie worked steadily through her morning. She answered the phone, scheduled deliveries, and she reviewed the emails that had been printed and mailed to her. She and her father agreed that there was no need to have a computer in the store, but they had found it useful to pay a monthly fee for website hosting and email monitoring.

Sadie thought that her father's solution had been quite smart: once a week or so, the Mennonite gentleman who set up and maintained their website sent copies of the emails that Ephrata Woodworks had received. Sadie carefully reviewed each email and handled what she could by phone, and she neatly wrote out her responses to send back to their email savvy Mennonite helper. By the time Sadie had wrapped up the stack of email inquiries, she glanced at the clock and saw that it was nearly lunchtime. Thinking about the way that the three of them always sat down to eat together, she realized just how awkward lunch with her father and Abram might be.

Hanging the sign in the window that alerted any customers that the store would re-open in half an hour, Sadie retrieved the lunch basket from the small refrigerator underneath the counter. She easily managed the basket that Abram had so awkwardly insisted on carrying for her that morning, and she walked across the yard toward the cool of the oak-shaded table beside the workshop.

She set three places at the wooden picnic table: three plates, three forks and knives, and three water glasses. She served up portions of cold fried chicken from the night before, and she added potato salad, green beans, and set aside the slices of rhubarb pie that she'd brought for dessert.

Sadie picked up the pitcher and went into the workshop to let the men know that lunch was ready and fill the pitcher with cold well water. As she carried the pitcher back from the sink in the workshop, Sadie saw that Abram had waited for her. She looked up at him with a question in her blue eyes, but all he did was meet her gaze and hold the door open for her.

The three workers who made up Ephrata Woodworks sat down in the shade for their lunch, and they all bowed their heads to pray silently. As usual, there was little conversation. Samuel asked his daughter for another piece of chicken, and Abram helped himself to another spoonful of green beans. Sadie kept water glasses filled, and they companionably enjoyed the sunny spring day. When Samuel had finished his lunch, he rose from the table and announced that he planned to take a brief nap. While Samuel didn't always nap during the workday, he had a cushion-covered bench in a back room of the shop that he sometimes used for a quick catnap.

Abram and Sadie looked at one another. They were finally alone with time to speak privately. Sadie started to stand and collect the dishes from lunch, but Abram gently laid his hand on her arm. "Can I speak to you, Sadie?" he quietly asked.

"Of course," Sadie replied, as she sat back down at the table. "Is something troubling you, Abram?" she inquired, knowing full well what he wanted to discuss.

"Sadie, I," he said, and he stopped. Abram took a deep breath, looked into Sadie's lovely blue eyes, and spilled his thoughts. "I found your book. It was in the paperwork for my father. I didn't know what to do, and I hid it." All of Abram's words just tumbled out, and he paused to take a breath and looked at Sadie, willing her to say something to make the conversation easier for him.

As Abram waited, Sadie just held his gaze, not saying a word. He continued to fill the silence," I didn't know the book was yours at first, but I know your handwriting. I thought to give it to my father because I know that if you're hiding your book, then you must be doing something God wouldn't want you to." Abram paused to give Sadie a chance to say something…anything.

Sadie sat motionless. She'd decided to let him have his say and not interrupt the righteous indignation she knew was sure to come.

"I waited and prayed to God for an answer about what to do, and I'm still not sure. I read some of your writing, and I thought I understood why you hid the book. You write about the Englishers all the time. You waste your busy work hours thinking about people who live too much in the world, and you know you shouldn't," Abram declared. He heard himself speaking more harshly than he intended, but he couldn't help himself. If Sadie would only say something and stop his rambling!

Abram carried on, "Think of what the bishop would say, Sadie. Think of what your father would say if he knew that you were wasting time at work to scribble in your little book. Scribble about the Englishers. What would God say?" Feeling as if he were being swept along by a flood of words he couldn't control, Abram finally fell silent. He folded his hands, placed them in his lap, and promised himself that he wouldn't utter another word until Sadie said *something*.

A bit taken aback despite her calm expression, Sadie's mind raced. She thought about all of the things she could say to Abram. She couldn't decide if he was right – that she really shouldn't be secretly writing – or if he was dead wrong and involved in a matter that was really none of his business. And what gave him the right to be all high and mighty about her journal? Before she finally spoke, Sadie reminded herself that she needed to stay calm and keep her temper under control.

"Abram," she began. "First of all, you should not have read my private writing. And second, you have no business telling me what God wants me to be doing." Sadie's eyes flashed as she began to get a little worked up. "You are not the bishop, and you are not my father. You will give me my journal back, and you will mind your own business."

Sadie moved to stand up again, and Abram once again halted her with a light touch on her arm. She could feel the heat of his fingers through her lightweight sleeves. She sat again, took a deep breath, and waited for his response.

"Sadie, I know I'm not your father, but I am worried about you. Why would you write in secret?" he asked.

"Because I knew that you would all think that it's wrong for me to write!" Sadie exclaimed. "But it's not, and I want my book back," she finished flatly.

"Well I don't have it here," Abram explained. "I left it at home. I hadn't decided if I should show it to my father or your father yet."

"Abram," Sadie said with eyes flashing dangerously. "You will return my book. It's not right for you to keep something that doesn't belong to you. You will bring it back to me tomorrow."

"Well, Sadie, I will have to think on it," Abram finished. "I will pray for guidance, because I'm not sure that you're not doing wrong, and I can't stand by and watch you sin some more. God would want me to help you do the right thing."

"Abram Byler, you haughty, arrogant fool," Sadie countered. "You will bring me my journal. How do you know that I'm not writing because God wants me to?" Sadie began packing up the remnants of lunch and stacking dishes to wash before stowing them in the basket to go back to the Zook's house.

All Abram could manage was a puzzled stare at Sadie's shoulders as she put the basket on her arm and lifted the plates and forks to carry them inside. He meekly asked, "Do you need any help?"

Sadie didn't say a word, but briskly walked inside the shop to clean up. Abram Byler needed to learn his lesson, one way or another, she thought. She'd not speak to him again until he made things right and returned her journal.

Chapter Four

For the second night in a row, Abram hurried through his chores and went to bed early. His thoughts were a swirl of Sadie's writing, her words, and her lovely blue eyes. He needed some quiet time to himself to think. All cleaned up, Abram sat quietly on the edge of his bed, his hands on his knees. What should he make of this suddenly strong-willed young woman who seemed to be occupying his every waking thought? He knew that to be distracted from his work by frivolous things was wrong, but he couldn't get Sadie out of his head. Perhaps if he just read through her book and returned it to her, he would be able to move on. Retrieving the little volume from beneath his pillow, Abram settled in to read. He decided to start at the end and read the entries beginning with the most recent first.

Today a family came into the store. A tall, kindly father, a slender and stylish mother, and their two children – a girl of sixteen and anther girl of twelve. The family was looking for new bedroom furniture for the youngest girl. They explained that she wanted an "old fashioned" look for her room. They live in Maryland and decided to take a day trip to see "Amish Country." They were very friendly, and the girls were polite.

The youngest girl was so fascinated by my clothes. She kept trying to sneak a look at my bonnet while I wasn't looking, and she was so closely examining my dress and apron that I could tell that she was trying to see if I used buttons or pins to fasten my clothing. She was not trying to be rude, but she was certainly curious! I couldn't think of a way to talk about fastening my clothes in a way that would be modest – especially with a man in the room, so I didn't say anything.

They settled on a bed frame and two dressers for the young girl. I can't imagine having enough clothing to fill two dressers. I can't imagine wanting to have enough clothing to fill two dressers. The laundry alone must take forever! I thought about what this young girl would think if she could see my room, with its plain bed and simple pegs to hold all of my dresses, skirts, aprons, and blouses. I wonder if she would think me as strange as I thought her.

I sat down with the parents to write up the order. The bed and dressers would have to be custom made, and I was explaining the terms of the deposit and how long I expected it would take my father to make the furniture. The door opened and Nathan Kobel came inside. Nathan is the oldest son of the Mennonite family that lives down the road from us. He's smart, and I've heard that he's gotten a scholarship to a big university. I haven't talked to him often, but he's always very polite and respectful, even if he is very different from Plain folk.

As soon as he walked through the door, the oldest daughter of the family couldn't take her eyes off him. I guess he's the sort of man that worldly girls would be interested in. He was wearing faded blue jeans and a bright red shirt with a collar and one of those Polo horses embroidered on it. The sixteen-year-old girl was staring at him like she'd never seen a handsome young man before.

Nathan apologized for the interruption, and explained that his mother had asked him to drop by the store to ask if she could borrow one of my mother's sewing machines for a few days. Nathan's mother does a busy mail order business for hand made clothing, quilts, and curtains, and she was expecting some women on the next Sunday afternoon to help her with a big order. I told Nathan that I was sure it would be fine, and he offered to come by later in the week to pick up the sewing machine. He asked if I would be at home on Friday evening, and he asked if I had a need for a ride to run errands. His family has three cars, and they are always happy to help if we need a ride further than our buggies

*will take us. I told Nathan that I would check
with Da and Mama to see if we had a need to run
any errands. I thanked Nathan, and as he walked
out, the oldest girl looked at me with a surprised
expression.*

Abram let the book fall to his lap. What was Sadie thinking, he wondered. He knew the Kobel family, of course, and he'd always thought of Nathan Kobel as exactly the sort person who set the example of why being worldly was bad. He drove fast, and he was so friendly and easy when he talked to everyone, whether they were English, Amish, male, or female. Abram knew that jealousy was a sin, but he had always felt envious of Nathan's comfort and ease in every situation. And college? How could Sadie even think of spending time with Nathan? Surely Samuel and Hannah would have the sense to see the danger in letting Sadie run around with this Nathan.

Abram hurriedly picked up the little book with a panicked look on his face. He flipped through the pages of Sadie's neat writing until he found what he was looking for. Friday. If Sadie had written this entry this week, then she would be expecting Nathan tomorrow evening. Abram quickly raced through all of the possibilities. Sadie could be a sensible, good girl and refuse to go anywhere with the flashy Nathan Kobel. That was, of course, what she should do.

But what if Sadie didn't do what she should? What if Sadie's parents trusted this Mennonite snake and what if Sadie was too innocent to see the dangers in spending time with him? What if Nathan wanted to do more than simply take Sadie to run errands? What if he wanted to corrupt her? What if he wanted to teach her the ways of the world and the sinful things that happened at college?

Abram sat up straight in bed, the little book falling to the floor in his panic. Abram had to do something. He had to make Sadie see that she was in great danger, that her soul was at risk. She should know better than to play with the fire that was Nathan Kobel, but if she couldn't see the danger on her own, then Abram would have to show her. Abram had to talk to Sadie, and he would have to do it as soon as she arrived at the shop in the morning.

As Abram bent to pick up Sadie's book from the floor, he looked at the green journal. Now he was certain that it was wrong for Sadie to hide her writing and keep her secrets from her family and friends. If people like Nathan Kobel captured her attention, then surely she was dwelling on things that she shouldn't be. Surely her writing was a sin. Surely Sadie would understand that he only had her soul and her best interests at heart. Abram hid the book for a second evening and hoped that he could make Sadie understand that his keeping it was really for her own good. That's how God would want it.

After a restless night, Abram awoke with a plan to take care of two problems at once. He didn't want Sadie spending time with that worldly Nathan Kobel, and he needed time to talk to Sadie about her book. Abram decided that the best way to handle this situation was by being open and honest. He would tell his parents that he wanted to talk to Sadie Zook that evening, and he was sure that if he showed up at the Zook farm on a Friday night that he'd be invited to stay for dinner with the family. He could also count on being asked to stay after for games with the family and maybe even a chance to ask Sadie to go for a walk after dinner. The more he thought about Sadie, the more Abram found himself unable to think about anything else. While he would never want to court a girl who wrote so fondly of such worldly people, Abram started to wonder if he'd find other girls a little dull compared to Sadie.

Abram did his morning chores, told his parents that he would be going to the Zooks for dinner, and hitched his horse to his buggy for his drive to town. On his quiet drive, he decided that perhaps Sadie needed a softer touch than he'd been able to pull off before. He resolved to be less judgmental and more understanding. Abram was a little surprised to be looking forward to seeing Sadie at work in just a few hours.

❄ ❄ ❄

Sadie awoke, and her first thought was of her journal – her journal in the hands of tall, dark, and full of himself Abram Byler. As she started her morning routine, Sadie hoped that Abram would be reasonable, hand off the journal, and forget about his ethical quandary. After all, who did he think he was that he had any right to decide if Sadie's writing went against God's wishes? Sadie was quite comfortable with having reasoned out that God wouldn't have made her a writer if he didn't want her to exercise that talent. Well, she was mostly comfortable.

As Sadie got dressed and ready for the day, she thought about Abram and wondered why he'd take such an interest in her all of the sudden. He was concerned about the journal of course, but why hadn't he just given it back to her and let the matter drop? Perplexed by Abram's behavior, Sadie went downstairs to help her mother get breakfast ready.

When Sadie walked into the kitchen, she was surprised to find it dark and empty. Ever since she could remember, her mother was always the first person up and about in the morning, and Sadie was accustomed to coming downstairs to the smell of fresh coffee and fresh bread in the oven. Something was definitely wrong this morning.

Sadie crossed the kitchen and looked outside to see if her father and brothers were outside in the barn. She saw the door to the barn ajar, and the bright light shining inside told her that her father was milking their cows while her brothers mucked out stalls and fed the horses. Grabbing a wrap to ward of the morning's chill, Sadie hurried to the barn, worried about where her mother might be.

"Da?" Sadie called as she entered the barn. "What is wrong? Where's Mama?"

Samuel looked up from his milking stool and answered. "Don't worry, Sadie. I didn't want to wake you. Hannah is sick, and she went back to bed. I told her that you and Miriam could handle breakfast and getting Esther off to school."

Sadie exhaled with relief. "Oh good," she sighed. "I'm

sorry Mama's not feeling good, but I'll go wake Miriam and we'll handle things this morning." As she turned to go back to the house, Sadie stopped and asked," Can you manage the shop without me today, Da? Friday is Mama's baking day, and I can stay home and make sure it gets done."

"Hannah would like that, and Abram and I can manage just fine," Samuel answered. "You're a good girl, Sadie, and a big help to your mother and me." Samuel smiled at his daughter, and turned his attention back to his work.

Sadie walked back to the house thinking of the work she had planned to accomplish at the store today. She could send her father with a list of customers who were expecting calls, and the rest of the work could wait until Monday. Sadie remembered with a smile that her father had managed the store for years without her help. She figured that one day wouldn't put him out of business.

When Sadie happily returned to the warm kitchen, Miriam was humming to herself while she mixed up apple cinnamon bread. Sausages sizzled on the stove, and the kitchen smelled comforting and delicious. "Have you talked to Mama?" Sadie asked as she hung up her wrap and prepared to help her sister prepare breakfast.

"Yes, poor thing," Miriam replied as she poured the mixture into the loaf pan and opened the oven. "She's running a fever and feels just terrible. She said that if she doesn't feel better by tomorrow morning, she'll go see Dr. Higgins." Miriam rinsed her hands in the sink and started peeling potatoes for hash browns. "I told her that I would stay home to help her if I didn't have tests scheduled for most of my students today."

Miriam taught at the Amish school that was just a few miles away, and even though she didn't expect to teach more than another year or two before she had a home and children of her own to care for, Miriam was a dedicated and demanding teacher.

Looking across the kitchen at Sadie, Miriam asked, "Do you think Da could spare you for the day? I'm afraid that Mama will need to get to the doctor sooner than tomorrow, and even if she can rest and feel better, she'll worry that the baking won't get done."

"Da and I talked, and that's what we decided," Sadie answered. "Goodness knows Mama has taken care of us enough times when we've been sick. If I have time I'll even make some of her chicken and rice soup if she's hungry.

The girls worked together easily, preparing breakfast and lunches for the family members who would be heading out for work and school. It was while Miriam was laughing and recounting the story of the time that she'd been so sick and her fever so high that she'd mistaken her father for a terrifying bearded monster that Sadie remembered Abram and her journal. She'd been so busy and caught up in the day's changing plans that she'd forgotten that Abram should be arriving at work later that morning, and she'd been quite clear that he should have her book to return.

Surely, she thought, he'd have the sense to keep the book until he could return it to her personally. She hoped that he wouldn't hand it off to her father. Sadie didn't want to have to answer another round of questions about her writing. Even though Sadie had spent considerable time and thought deciding whether God would want her to keep her journal, and even though she felt comfortable with her decision that she was using a talent given to her by God, she wasn't at all confident that other Plain folk would feel the same way. She knew that she'd be better off if no one else knew.

As she cracked an egg too vigorously and began to pick out the shells that resulted from her little display of temper, Sadie told herself that fretting about Abram's having found the journal was a waste of her time and energy. What was done was done, and there was nothing to be gained by wishing she could change the past. All she could do was move forward and know that God would work things out in His own way. Working quickly through the rest of the eggs she was about to scramble, Sadie was surprised to discover that she felt a little disappointed that she wouldn't see Abram later that day. In spite of his frustrating, stern manner, she found that she'd been looking forward to another conversation with him. How peculiar, she thought, that the young man she'd previously given little thought to, was now on her mind and refusing to go away. She supposed that she'd just have to wait for Sunday, when she'd see him at the Stoltzfos house for their worship service.

As if Miriam had been reading her mind, Sadie's elder sister interrupted her thoughts. "I expect that Luke will offer to drive me home from church on Sunday," Miriam began, a little dreamy smile on her face. "Do you plan to let anyone drive you home this week?" Miriam asked.

"Well that all depends," Sadie replied with a smirk. "If Jacob Stoltzfos asks again, then I'll be riding home with Mama and Pa this week. He only wanted to talk about his buggy and how much it had cost him. Not only is he proud, but he always smells sour, like he needs to brush his teeth," Sadie laughed. "He's nothing like his brother Luke. You seem pretty sure that he'll ask you again, Miriam. Is there an understanding that we should know about?" Sadie asked, with a wide-eyed false innocence.

"Sadie Zook, that's absolutely none of your business, "Miriam replied primly. "There's nothing to tell, and until there is, I'll thank you for keeping your mind on your own business." Miriam dried her hands and glanced at Sadie with a good-humored grin that belied the sharp tone of her words. "I'll go wake Esther and check on Mama," she said as she headed to the stairs.

The rest of the morning passed in typical fashion, but for Hannah's absence. Miriam had reported that she was asleep and thought it best to let her get all the rest she could. Young Samuel and Isaac headed off to the Joseph Lapp's farm where both boys had worked since they left school after eighth grade. As the oldest Lapp boy had married and worked in his father-in-law's dairy, Samuel was Joseph's right hand and some day hoped to buy a piece of the Lapp farm for his own. Isaac, as the youngest man there, was usually given the least important and dirtiest jobs, but his sunny disposition allowed him to work a full day with a smile and sleep well at night knowing that he'd been an integral part of running a successful farm.

Miriam and Esther set off in the opposite direction for the school that Miriam taught and Esther attended. Though she was young, Esther was a bright girl and had decided that she wanted to be a teacher like Miriam and like their mother, Hannah, had been. The girls chattered about the history lesson of the day before and Miriam answered Esther's questions about why Plain people spoke Pennsylvania German and English, while Englishers typically only spoke one language. Before the girls knew it, they'd covered the three miles to school.

After Sadie got her family on their respective ways, she tiptoed upstairs to check on Hannah. "Mama?" she whispered at the bedroom doorway. Seeing Hannah turn toward her, Sadie crossed the room to sit on the bed next to her mother. "How are you feeling?" Sadie asked as she reached out her hand to smooth Hannah's damp hair from her forehead. "My goodness, Mama, you're burning up," Sadie quietly exclaimed. "Let me get you a cool cloth."

"Thank you, sweet girl," Hannah replied. "You'll make a wonderful wife and mother one day."

"Mama, you've taught us by your example," Sadie replied. "Do you remember how sick Miriam was?"

"When she screamed and tried to jump out of bed to get away from your Da?" Hannah started to laugh. Hannah's laugh turned into a cough and she leaned back on her pillows. "Sadie, will you bring me some water? And an extra quilt? I feel so cold."

"Of course, Mama. Be still and I'll be right back."

Sadie unfolded the bear paw quilt that was the very first that all of the Zook girls had worked on together. As she smoothed her hand over the block that had been Esther's very first, with the contrasting navy and fuchsia solid cotton fabric and the tiny mistake that Esther had been so unhappy about, Sadie realized that if she had time later in the day, she wanted to write about the afternoon that she and her sisters had worked on this very quilt. Maybe while the pies were in the oven and the bread was rising, Sadie could find the time to record her memories of that day from just a few months before.

When Sadie had tucked her mother in, cooled her forehead with the damp cloth, and gotten her to drink some water, Hannah drifted off to sleep. Sadie watched her mother, thinking of the thousands of ways in which Hannah had taught her by example what it meant to be a good woman, wife, and mother. Hoping that Hannah would wake in a few hours and feel better, Sadie quietly left the room and pulled the door closed behind her.

❊ ❊ ❊

All of the muscles across Abram's broad shoulders strained as he and Samuel lifted the solid oak dresser onto the huge box truck that was backed up to the door of the wood shop. "Samuel, I'm surely glad that we don't have to deliver this bedroom set," Abram declared as he wiped the sweat from beneath the broad brim of his hat. "Can you imagine how the delivery company will get all of this up to the sixteenth floor?" he asked.

"I am very glad that we don't have to figure that

out, Abram," Samuel laughed. "It's plenty of trouble just getting it on this truck"

Samuel had figured out years before that the logistics of delivery were better handled by Englishers, and he'd found a local Ephrata company that he trusted to make sure that the furniture that he had labored over would be handled with care. The fact that Samuel didn't have to coordinate the delivery of an oak wardrobe, bed, and two dressers to a Manhattan high-rise was worth the expense of his valuable contractor. Samuel had learned long ago that it was best to focus your labor on the tasks God had made you suited for and to find people with talents in other areas to do the work that Samuel wasn't built for.

As the two men loaded the last of the pieces to go out for delivery, Abram thought for what seemed like the thousandth time that day about the blonde, blue-eyed girl that he was surprised to discover that he missed. How was it that a girl who he'd never thought a whole lot about had consumed his attention? He'd been shocked to discover that not only had he looked forward to seeing her, but that he'd been bitterly disappointed that Samuel had arrived at Ephrata Woodworks without that girl whose eyes were the same color as the gorgeous June sky.

Deciding that he simply couldn't wait another two days – until the Sunday church gathering at the Stoltzfos farm, Abram was determined to find a way to ever so casually invite himself to the Zooks. Assuring himself that his greatest concern was that Nathan Kobel not have the chance to prey on innocent Sadie, Abram cleared his throat before addressing Samuel.

"Sir, if your wife is still sick this evening, I would be happy to keep an eye on the boys and help with the chores if you need to take her to see the doctor," Abram offered. As he was speaking, he wondered why it was so much easier for him to talk to Samuel than Sadie. He knew that he was a smart and steady fellow, but every single time he opened his mouth in front of Sadie, he felt as though his thoughts and words became hopelessly tangled and emerged from his mouth in an embarrassing, jumbled heap.

Samuel thought for a moment, and nodded at Abram. "That's kind of you to offer. Young Samuel and Isaac would be glad of the help, I'm sure." He paused and continued, "Even if we don't have to make a trip to town, you can stay for dinner. I'm sure that Sadie will have made a few special dishes since she doesn't usually have a full day at home in the kitchen."

"Samuel, I'm glad to be able to help. Perhaps we should wrap up a bit early so that you can make it home before dark," Abram suggested, thinking that he would love to get Sadie to agree to a walk on what looked to be a lovely evening. Sadie outside on a warm, late spring evening. Outside with a breeze that might catch the edge of her bonnet and allow a few tendrils of hair to escape. Blonde hair in the breeze…

Abram shook his head to shake off his daydream, and he realized that Samuel was looking at him as if he expected a response. "Sir?" he asked. "I'm sorry. I was thinking about whether I can finish the table for…" Abram's voice trailed off, and he looked sheepishly at

Samuel. "Truthfully, Samuel, I was daydreaming. What did you ask?"

"It doesn't matter, son," Samuel replied with a laugh. He knew that look on Abram's face all too well. If Samuel were a betting man, he'd have put money on Abram's thoughts being on a bonnet rather than balsam wood. There weren't very many topics that could make a young man's thoughts drift as far and as happily as Abram's had clearly gone. "Let's get back to work so we can get home and enjoy Sadie's cooking."

Chapter Five

As much as she enjoyed the challenge of keeping up with her father's successful business, Sadie had thoroughly enjoyed her domestic day at home. She'd baked four loaves of multigrain bread, two loaves of cinnamon raisin swirl bread, and two rhubarb pies. She'd also made the dough for the pizza she was planning on serving for their Friday night dinner, and she'd stacked some kindling and firewood next to their outside oven. They usually used the oven when they had bigger than usual meals to prepare, but it was handiest during the summer when the ovens inside made the house miserably hot. She thought the wood-fired pizzas would be an unexpected treat when her family returned home from work and school.

As Sadie chopped tomatoes, peppers, onions, and mushrooms for pizza toppings, she glanced at the clock and thought she might just have enough time to sit for a little while and write a few words. She finished up the vegetables, washed and dried her hands, and decided to head upstairs to check on Hannah before she relaxed.

As she eased the door open quietly, she noticed right away that the sheets and quilts were a tangled mess. Her mother was still asleep, but clearly quite restless. Hannah's eyes opened as Sadie entered the room.

"I don't feel good," she said hoarsely. "Will you get me some more water and some aspirin?"

"Of course, Mama," Sadie answered. "Are you hungry? I can reheat some soup for you," she offered.

"No, sweet girl. I don't feel like eating," Hannah replied. "What time is it? I think I may need to go see Doctor Higgins when your father gets home. I think my temperature is higher."

"Do you want me to drive you into town, Mama," Sadie asked. "It may be several hours before Da gets home."

"No, no," Hanna answered. "I'm not going to die. I just think I need an antibiotic."

"Okay, Mama. I'll go get your aspirin and water. Need anything else?"

"No thank you, Sadie. I'll just get some more sleep. Is the baking going okay? Any problems?"

"Not a single one, Mama. Breads are done, and so are the pies. I made pizza dough too. I thought I'd cook outside tonight since it's going to be such a lovely evening.

"Good. I'm sure your brothers and sisters will enjoy it, even if Da and I aren't here."

Sadie supplied her mother with water and aspirin, smoothed out the bedclothes, and tucked her mother back in. She stopped by her room on her was downstairs

to fetch a little blank notebook that she'd set aside for just
an occasion as this one. Typically the Zook house was full
of people, chatter, and laughter. There was rarely peace
and quiet, and there was rarely any privacy. Sadie had
every intention of taking advantage of both things today.

Settling in the rocking chair in the corner of the
sitting room, Sadie put her feet on the footstool, rested
her fresh journal on her knees, and began to write.

*I was reminded today of Esther's first quilt – well we
all worked on it, but it was the very first time that
she made a block all on her own and helped with the
entire quilt. It was a bear paw pattern, and we had
each picked our colors for out blocks. We let Esther
choose first since she hadn't worked on a quilt before.
She'd done plenty of mending and had even helped
with the last bunch of aprons we'd made, but she
was very excited. She picked out a beautiful dark
blue, and she found a small remainder bundle of the
brightest fuchsia. She was right – the colors looked
perfect together.*

*It was a Sunday afternoon – one of the weeks that
we didn't go to church services – so many people
think that Plain folk go to church every day, but
really we only go every other Sunday. And we don't
have a church building. We take turns holding
services in our homes. Anyway, Esther and Mama
were working closely and slowly since Esther didn't
have the years of experience that Miriam and I
did. Miriam and I sat in the warm sunshine – nice*

because it was a cold winter day. We talked about her students and my work at Da's shop.

We'd been working for quite a while, and I remember that Miriam was laughing at one of my stories about Englisher customers in Da's shop, when we realized that Esther had started crying. Mama was trying to calm her down, but she was very upset. When I asked her what was wrong, she didn't even talk, but she handed me the nearly finished quilt square she'd been working so hard on. The mistake was obvious. She'd not lined up the very last pieces of fabric correctly, and the corner of the block was crooked.

I thought back to the mistakes I had made when I was younger and first able to help the older ladies with big quilting projects, and I smiled to myself. I realized that the lesson that Esther was about to learn was one the every Plain woman learns at one time or another. I put my arm around Esther's shoulder and explained to her the very same thing my mother had explained to me and to Miriam. I told her that our mistakes remind us to stay modest and humble. Believing that we can create something that's perfect is mocking God and being proud. I told her that every single person makes mistakes because we're imperfect and need God for our salvation.

I held up her hand-stitched square and told her that every time she sees that square that it can be a gentle reminder that we're not perfect. Only God is perfect.

*We should obey Him and try to be better people,
but trying to be perfect is a sign of pride. Esther
understood and cheered up. She'd been so worried
about spoiling the beautiful quilt that she'd forgotten
the lessons that we can learn from everything we do.
I showed her the square I was working on, and it
wasn't hard to pick out some of the tiny stitches that
weren't perfectly even. Mama and Miriam showed
her their tiny mistakes too. Esther learned that
handmade isn't perfect, and that accepting our flaws
keeps us humble.*

Sadie closed her new journal and thought about what she'd just written. She knew in her heart and soul that what she'd just written wasn't wrong. God wouldn't be displeased with her. After all, she was using her writing as a devotional in a way. It helped her to find a quiet time to reflect on what she could learn from the events in her life and how to be a better person. She wondered for a moment if perhaps Abram had found her journal for a reason. She knew that God had a plan for everyone, and she thought that maybe she and Abram had been pushed into this uncomfortable relationship for a reason. Thinking a moment more, Sadie opened the little book again and wrote a few more lines.

*Abram, I thought of you after I wrote this passage,
and I wanted you to read it. If you have thoughts on
what I've written, I would welcome your response.
You can write in this book and bring it to me when I
see you next.*

Sadie closed the book and decided that she'd done the right thing. She thought that Abram might even find some of the same peace that Sadie found in writing down thoughts and feelings about everyday events.

Though she had enjoyed her little break from the workday, Sadie was surprised to find that she'd been looking forward to seeing Abram and was a bit sorry that she would have to wait until Sunday's church service to see him. She knew there would be far too many people around for a private conversation.

The clock in the dining room chimed three o'clock, and Sadie realized that Miriam and Esther would be home in less than an hour. The school day ended at three-thirty, and Sadie figured that if she washed a few towels and aprons that Esther could help her hang the clothes to dry while Miriam reviewed her students' work and prepared her lessons for Monday. Da would be home around five-thirty, and she'd have dinner ready around six. Sadie put her journal away, checked on Hannah, and got started on laundry.

Sadie had just wrung out the last of the aprons and towels when she heard her sisters return home. She hoisted the laundry basket to her hip, grabbed the bag of clothespins, and went out to greet the girls.

"How was school, Esther?" Sadie asked. "Was your teacher mean and spiteful?"

"Miriam gave us homework over the weekend!" Esther exclaimed. "But it's only a little bit, and I like the book we're reading, so I guess it's not too awful."

"If you and Hanna Lapp hadn't been whispering and

giggling in class, you would have finished your work and you wouldn't have homework," Miriam reminded her sister. "How's Mama feeling?" she asked Sadie.

"Not so good. She thinks she may need to go see the doctor when Da gets home. I offered to take her myself, but she said she could wait. We have a treat for dinner! We'll make pizza outside. It's going to be such a lovely evening that I thought we could sit outside. Esther and I can make the pizza while you get caught up on work."

"That sounds wonderful," Miriam replied enthusiastically. "It would be nice to finish all of my work so that I don't have to rush home after church on Sunday."

Sadie nodded at Esther, telling her, "Run in and put your school books away and come help me hang up the laundry to dry. After that, we'll start on dinner."

Ester skipped inside and returned, ready to help Sadie. Holding the cloth bag with the clothespins, Esther handed the pins to Sadie as they worked their way down the clothesline, chatting happily.

Sadie was surprised when she heard a wagon approaching the house, and when it came into view from the road behind the barn, she stopped her work. She set the basket of clothes on the picnic table and walked toward her father's wagon.

"What's wrong Da?" she called out as he turned the corner. Sadie worried that perhaps Samuel was feeling sick as well.

"Nothing is wrong, my dear. Abram and I just decided to end work a little early so that we could enjoy the wonderful dinner that I'm sure you have planned."

"Abram?" Sadie asked, looking up the road without seeing another soul.

"He'll be along shortly," Samuel explained. "He offered to stop by and help the boys with the chores if I need to take Hannah to the doctor. How is she feeling?"

"Abram offered to help?" Sadie repeated, perplexed.

"Yes, Abram," Samuel said with a hint of smile just barely visible above his beard. "And your Mama? How is she?"

"Oh, Da, I'm sorry. She isn't feeling good at all and thinks that she needs to go to the doctor. She's been in bed all day, and her temperature was pretty high the last time I checked on her. Make sure you tell Doctor Higgins that she took some aspirin."

"Well the boys will be glad of the help with the chores, and I suspect that Abram will be glad of one of your meals," Samuel said with a straight face. Typically, he tried to appear oblivious to the goings on between his children and the objects of their interest, but he couldn't ignore the signs of a growing attraction between Sadie and Abram. He wondered how long it would be before the two admitted their interest to themselves, let alone each other.

"Abram. Hm. I guess I better prepare for an extra place at dinner," Sadie said under her breath as she walked back to the house. Wondering if Abram would have her journal, Sadie washed her hands and prepared to get her chopped vegetables from the refrigerator. She stopped short, though, when she looked out the window and realized that she'd stranded Esther with the rest of the laundry to hang. She darted outside to discover that her resourceful little sister had pulled a step ladder from the barn and was laboriously moving the ladder to hang each piece of wet laundry, all while holding the bag of clothespins in her mouth.

"Esther, you're an angel! You could have called for me and I would have come back out," Sadie called from the doorway.

Removing the clothespins from her mouth, Esther answered, "I can do it by myself, Sadie."

Sadie was about to answer her sister when she heard another buggy approaching the farm. Sure enough, Abram's little buggy rounded the barn, and without even realizing it, Sadie reached up to smooth her hair and tuck the few wispy, stray pieces back beneath her prayer cap where they belonged. Straightening her apron, Sadie turned to go back inside. She stopped, put her hands to her suddenly flushed cheeks and sternly told herself to calm down.

Taking a deep breath, Sadie began her calm, measured walk across to the barn. She hoped that she looked calmer than she felt.

"Abram Byler," she called. "Da told me you would be along shortly."

Abram pulled his horse up next to the barn and began to clamber out of the buggy. "Well, I thought it might be some help to the boys to be here for the chores if Samuel had to go to town with Hannah," Abram said stiffly. He wondered how to continue and decided just to forge ahead while he had Sadie to himself. "I read more of your book, and Sadie, you need to be careful. You don't know how dangerous it can be to dwell on things of the world. We are separate for a reason, and…" Abram's voice trailed off as he saw the cloud of dust and heard the engine that could only mean that an automobile approached the farm.

"Oh dear!" exclaimed Sadie. "I completely forgot to tell Mama that Nathan was stopping by this evening." Stepping back toward Abram's buggy to make room for Nathan to pull in, Sadie stumbled over Abram's foot and lost her balance.

"Sadie!" Abram exclaimed as he grabbed her elbow with one hand and steadied her with his other hand at her waist. He didn't remember ever having been quite so close to Sadie before, and her intoxicating, warm cinnamon scent was even stronger than usual since she'd spent the day baking. Helping Sadie to regain her balance, Abram gently held her elbow and waist a little longer than necessary and was reluctant to let go of this lovely young woman in his arms. Thinking that Nathan had perfectly awful timing, Abram slowly removed his hands and let Sadie step away to a more appropriate distance.

As Sadie stepped away from Abram, she turned her head to look at him. The way he had touched her had felt different. It had felt sweet and warm and well, nice. Sadie couldn't think of another word, and she didn't often find herself at a loss for words. She continued to stare up at Abram, as he was considerably taller than she. She opened her mouth to say something, but she was interrupted by Nathan's cheerful call from his car window.

"Hey, Sadie!" he shouted. "Hey Abram. What's up, man?" Nathan unfolded his long legs from his metallic blue Toyota Camry and stretched as he closed the car door. He crossed the yard to shake Abram's hand and wink at Sadie. "What's goin' on, man?" Nathan asked Abram. "Long time, no see," he said casually.

""I am fine, thank you," Abram relied stiffly. "We are all fine," he elaborated, looking at Sadie to gauge her response to this ridiculously good-looking young man who wore his confidence and worldliness like a comfortable second skin. Abram felt a moment of envy for the young man who seemed to float in and out of every social setting without a care in the world.

"Hey, Sadie, my mom really appreciates your lending us a sewing machine," Nathan said as he approached Abram's buggy. Whistling, Nathan slid his hands over the shiny curves of the two-seater. "Wow, man," he exclaimed. "This baby is gorgeous."

"There's no need to make fun, Nathan," Abram replied. "Not all of us need flashy cars and expensive schooling. Some of us are content being Plain."

"No, no, Abram!" Nathan protested, leaning in and putting his hand on Abram's arm. "No, I mean it. She's a beautiful buggy. Just because I drive a car and am going away to school doesn't mean I can't appreciate a fine piece of work like this one. For real. She's gorgeous."

"Well," Abram answered gruffly. "I'm sure you have her top speed beat," he said with the start of a smile. "And thanks."

Sadie took the two young men's conversation in, and

looked at Abram with wide-eyed wonder. Had he just made a joke? Was it possible that there was more to this tall young man than simply a somber sense of duty? Sadie felt as though the day had just gotten a little bit brighter.

"Oh!" Sadie exclaimed. "I completely forgot to tell Mama that you were coming by for the sewing machine. She's been sick in bed all day, and I got so caught up in the baking that I completely forgot."

"Should I come back later," Nathan asked. "Do you need help? A ride to town?"

"The sewing machine is no trouble, and Da was going to take Mama in to town. Let me ask him if he would like a ride. Mama's been feeling so bad that a quicker trip will probably be better for her."

Sadie hurried inside and left Abram and Nathan outside. The two men looked at the buggy, sizing each other up out of the corners of their eyes. They'd know each other for years, but they hadn't been good friends. Nathan had always attended public school, played sports, and had goals far beyond the city limits of Ephrata, Pennsylvania. Abram had attended the little Amish school – the same one that Miriam now taught – and had left school after the eighth grade just like the rest of the Plain folk. Abram had been working ever since, and in some ways Nathan felt a little childish in comparison.

"You are here to borrow a sewing machine?" Abram asked.

"Yeah. My mom has a huge order that needs to be shipped out next week, so my aunt and some friends are coming over tomorrow to help out. Mom thought an extra machine would make the work go quicker."

"I am sure Hannah is happy to help a neighbor," said Abram solemnly. "And I'm sure your mother will be anxious to get to work. Shall I go see if Sadie has the machine so that you can be on your way?"

"Nah, no hurry," answered Nathan. "I may have a drive to town ahead of me if Mrs. Zook is really sick. I'm in no rush. To be honest, I thought I could maybe get an invitation to dinner. Looks like they're cooking outside tonight."

"Well as soon as young Samuel and Isaac get home, I'm going to help out with chores so that Samuel can take Hannah to the doctor. I don't know that Sadie will be expecting so many extra people for dinner. After all, she stayed home from work today because Mrs. Zook was too sick to do the baking."

"Oh come on, Abram," Nathan said, lightly elbowing him. "You know that the Zooks are happy to have anyone for dinner anytime. There's no reason why you should have all the fun. I mean it's not like you're Luke Stoltzfos, about to be part of the family, are you?"

Abram bristled. "Well of course not, and I'm sure Miriam Zook would thank you to keep your nose out of private matters that don't concern you."

"Good grief, man," Nathan countered. "It's not like you're a member of the family, are you? Unless you're sweet on Sadie or something…is that it?"

"Of course not! I just know that we don't need your sort poking your nose into our business. Giving Mrs.

Zook a ride to town is one thing. Acting like you're a part of the family is another."

"My sort? Really?" Nathan asked. "I believe the same things you do. I just think that I can believe in God without having to dress differently and having to leave school after eighth grade. We're not so different."

"I don't know how you can say that, Nathan. You don't even know me," Abram declared. "Look at you! You look no different from a boy who listens to rap music and uses drugs."

"Wow. Is that really how you see me?" asked Nathan. "Do you know how much grief I get in school because I'm a Mennonite? Do you know how hard it is to be faithful in the real world? You think you're so strong in your faith, but you haven't tested it like I have."

Nathan turned on his heel and headed for the house, muttering, "I'm going to see what's keeping Sadie."

Abram stood rooted to the ground. He stared after Nathan and couldn't even begin to sort out all of his thoughts. Full of questions, he stood and tried to work through what bothered him so much about the conversation he'd just had. Did Nathan really think the Plain living was taking the easy way out? And what did he mean about Abram and Sadie? Trying to decide whether or not he should follow Nathan into the house, Abram was spared the necessity of making a decision by the return home of Samuel and Isaac.

Chapter Six

Knocking and opening the kitchen door as he usually did, Nathan peered inside to see if the kitchen was occupied. Seeing that the usually bustling room was empty, he called a hello to anyone who might be in earshot.

"In here," Miriam called from the sitting room. She had her paperwork stacked in neat piles on the desk that the family shared. "Oh, hello, Nathan. Sadie said you'd be in for the sewing machine. Mama wanted to lend you her best – she's been having trouble with breaking needles in our older one."

"Mom wanted me to thank you. She's been so busy, and her helpers tomorrow will make all the difference to her."

"You're welcome, of course. It's no trouble at all, and it's good to help your neighbors. Speaking of that, I think Da is going to ask you for a ride to town. Mama's pretty sick, and the sooner we get her some medicine, the sooner she will feel better."

"Of course. I'm happy to help. We would never have gotten our hay baling finished before that big storm last year if your Da hadn't sent Samuel and Isaac over to help us finish. Just as the first drops were starting to fall, we'd just gotten it all done."

"Well just have a seat, Nathan. Da will be down in a minute. He and Sadie are getting her ready to go. Can I get you some lemonade while you wait?" Miriam asked.

"Don't trouble yourself, Miriam," he replied. "I can get it myself. I don't want to mess up your work."

Nathan went back into the kitchen and got himself a glass of lemonade. As he sipped the drink, he inhaled the amazing aroma of a kitchen that had yielded bread and pies. Warm, rich, and spicy smells filled the cheerful room. Noticing the bowls of sliced vegetables on the counter, Nathan called into the other room.

"Miriam, is dinner going to be pizza tonight? Any chance I can get an invite?

"Oh, Nathan, you don't have to ask, and you know it. Of course you can stay for dinner – as long as Mama's visit with the doctor doesn't take too long. And leftover pizza isn't terrible, anyway, is it?"

"Right on. Wood-fired pizza is awesome!"

Nathan brought his lemonade back into the sitting room and perused the bookshelves while Miriam continued her work. Before long, he heard footsteps descending from upstairs.

Hannah held Samuel's arm for support as they came into the sitting room. She looked tired and feverish, but she greeted Nathan with a tired smile.

"Did Miriam show you which sewing machine to take?"

"Yes ma'am. We sure appreciate it."

Samuel helped his wife toward the door as he spoke to Nathan. "Are you sure it's no trouble to take us to town?" he asked.

"None at all." Nathan winked at Miriam as he continued, "Miriam was kind enough to invite me to stay for dinner when we get back, if that's okay."

"You know you're always welcome here," Samuel replied. "Let's get going, if you don't mind. Hannah really feels terrible."

Samuel got Hannah settled in the back seat of the Camry, while Nathan carried the sewing machine outside. He hadn't thought about the fact that the treadle machine wouldn't possibly fit in the trunk of his car.

"Mr. Zook, after we get back, do you think you could send Samuel over to my house with the sewing machine in your wagon? I wasn't thinking about how big yours is compared with our electric machines."

Samuel laughed at the prospect of putting a sewing machine the size of a small piece of furniture into Nathan's car, and he assured the young man that they would give him a hand when they returned.

In the barn, the three young men had finished taking care of the animals, and Samuel and Isaac went outside to weed some of the garden. Hanna typically kept the neatest garden around, but since she'd been in bed all day, and since Sadie had been occupied with the baking, the boys thought that Hannah would appreciate a little garden maintenance. Abram had volunteered to help Sadie get the outdoor oven lit so that it could heat before dinner.

Abram was awkwardly stacking and restacking the wood that Sadie had placed by the oven when she came back outside.

"I thought you might need some help with the fire," he announced as he watched Sadie cross the yard. It occurred to Abram that although he'd seen Sadie nearly every day for several years of her life, he'd never really *looked* at her, never really paid attention.

"Well that's kind of you, Abram," Sadie replied.

The two of them carefully stacked the wood in the oven, taking their time to place each piece slowly and carefully. While they worked, Abram studied Sadie in a way he never had before. He was surprised to discover that there was the lightest dusting of freckles on her nose, and Abram was even more surprised to discover that he found them fetching.

"So…." Sadie said, indicating that she'd been waiting for him to say something. "My journal?" Sadie fixed him with her gaze.

"Well, about the journal," he paused. "I read more of it last night, and Sadie, I'm worried about you. You don't see how dangerous some of what you're writing about is. There's a reason Plain folk live separate from the world."

"Well of course there is," Sadie snapped. "But you have no right to keep something that belongs to me.

"But Sadie, I have your soul in mind. I want to do what is best for you."

"Abram Byler, we've been through this. You will give me back my book. You will, because it's the right thing to do."

"But Sadie, you don't understand."

"Oh, I understand just fine," she interrupted. "I understand that you have something that does not belong to you." Sadie stopped her tirade, and paused. "What if I could change your mind? What if I could show you something that would help you understand my writing better?"

Abram looked at Sadie's hand that was resting on the edge of the outdoor picnic table. He noticed that just under the cuff of her long sleeves were a few tiny freckles, just like the ones on her nose.

"Sadie, I would like to understand you better," he said quietly.

Without even knowing that his hand moved, Abram saw himself reach out and touch Sadie's wrist with one finger. Both silent, as if all the world's clocks had stopped and they were the only two people in the world, Abram moved his gaze from Sadie's freckled wrist, up along her arm, until his eyes met hers. They looked, really looked at one another, and Abram was the one to break the silence.

"Sadie, I don't want to argue with you. The only reason I'm worried is because, well,"

"Because what?" Sadie prompted.

"Because I"

Abram stopped short as Esther burst out of the kitchen door at a full run, her high-pitched scream drawing all attention to the barefoot girl running full-tilt toward Sadie and Abram

"Sadie!" she squealed. "Sadie, make him stop!"

There was no question to whom Esther referred. Isaac stood in the kitchen doorway with a wicked grin on his face and cupped hands that surely contained some vile specimen of beetle or snake he'd found in Hannah's garden.

Abram's face fell as Sadie turned to Esther and began trying to convince the girl that plotting revenge against her rotten brother wasn't the best way to handle him. Reminding Esther that God would punish evil brothers, and that she was better off ignoring Isaac, Sadie lightly swatted her sister and sent her back inside to start warming up the jars of tomato sauce that Hannah had made the year before. Isaac had wisely vanished and resumed his chores, and Sadie and Abram were once again alone, however briefly.

Glancing over at the garden to make sure that Isaac had returned to it and wasn't hiding and waiting to further torment his sister, Sadie turned back to face Abram.

Resolved to finish the conversation and speak his mind, Abram squared his shoulders, took a deep breath, and began.

"If I saw my brother or my sister doing something dangerous, I would stop them because I care about them. I want to keep bad things from happening to them, and it's my responsibility to step in and help them if I'm able."

Instantly indignant, Sadie sputtered, "Your sister? Your *brother*?" Sadie turned her back to Abram and couldn't say another word. She knew that she had no reason to be angry with Abram, but when he'd compared her to his siblings, she'd felt instantly hurt and disappointed. Could it be that she liked Abram more than she had realized? Hands on her hips, Sadie whirled to face the tall young man again.

"Your sister? Is that how you think of me?" she asked in a voice much calmer and less accusatory.

"I don't know why I said that, Sadie. How should I think of you?" he asked quietly. "I don't know why everything I say to you comes out all wrong. I have trouble thinking straight, and everything comes out all jumbled and awkward and stupid." Afraid to make eye contact, Abram looked at his shoes and held his breath waiting for Sadie's response.

Glancing around the yard to ensure that no one was watching the two of them, Sadie stepped toward Abram and put her hand on his muscled arm. Looking up into his eyes, she said, with a gleam in her own sky blue eyes, "I have the perfect solution. "

Puzzled, Abram watched the young woman turn and walk inside. He noticed that Sadie's walk was different from all the other girls he knew. He couldn't put his finger on what was different about it, but he discovered that he was looking forward to watching her and trying to figure it out. As Sadie reappeared and started toward him, Abram noticed that she held something carefully concealed beneath her apron.

"Here," she said, as she handed him her new journal. "Go put this in your buggy and read it when you get home. If you want to, you can answer it. There's plenty of space."

Mutely accepting the book, Abram stowed it safely in his buggy and returned to ask Sadie about the contents of the book.

"You will see," she said with a smile. "And I look forward to your response."

Brightly mentioning that Samuel, Hannah, and Nathan had been gone for quite a while, Sadie cheerfully suggested that Abram start the fire, and she went back inside.

Abram moved as if by rote, lighting a twist of newspaper and gently blowing on the kindling to coax it into catching fire. He didn't think he'd ever been so curious as he was about the book Sadie had given him. He was certain that it held more of her writing – it was the same size as the little green journal that he still had underneath his pillow. Though this book had a yellow fabric cover, he knew this was another of Sadie's journals.

He wondered what on earth she could have written. How many journals did one girl need? Surely even one was too many, and what did she mean about his answering her? She couldn't possibly expect him to write back, could she? Unless she thought of it like a letter…could she have written something just for him? Abram's mind was a jumble of blonde hair, blue eyes, tiny freckles, and Sadie's words. Only when the flames in the oven got close enough to his hand to distract him, did Abram realize that he'd been standing in front of the oven with a ridiculous grin on his face.

Straightening his hat, Abram looked around the yard for something productive to do. Noticing that Samuel and Isaac were still working in the garden, he walked over and offered to help finish up the weeding – anything so that he wasn't standing in the middle of the yard grinning like a fool.

Chapter Seven

In the kitchen, Sadie and Esther brewed fresh iced tea, made lemonade, and made sure all of the ingredients were ready for the pizzas so that they could be start dinner as soon as their parents returned from town. Miriam had just finished her schoolwork and walked into the kitchen to offer her help when the girls heard Nathan's car pull into the drive.

"I'll help Mama get settled while you girls start dinner," Miriam offered as she opened the kitchen door to admit Samuel and Hannah. "What did the doctor say, Mama?" she asked.

"It is strep throat. I should feel better by Sunday, he seemed to think," Hannah answered. "And as much as I hate to miss Sadie's pizza, I'm going back to bed. Can you girls handle everything?"

"Of course, Mama," both Sadie and Miriam answered in unison.

"Esther already volunteered to do all of the dishes," Sadie continued, with a wink at her mother.

Hannah left the kitchen with Miriam and Samuel to help her upstairs and get her settled in for the evening. Even though her throat felt like it was on fire, she smiled as she listened to her two youngest girls' good-natured teasing.

Sadie and Esther started their pizza preparation. Sadie stretched and worked the dough into a smooth, round circle and placed it on a wooden paddle that had been liberally dusted with cornmeal. Esther spread tomato sauce and topped with mozzarella cheese made from the milk of their own cows. By the time Esther had finished, Miriam had returned to the kitchen to load the pizzas up with fresh vegetables. One by one, the pizzas were transferred to the outdoor oven. The girls set the two picnic tables outside, and dinner was ready.

Esther rang the dinner bell that told the boys in the garden and barn that it was time to wash up and come eat. While young Samuel, Isaac, and Abram washed their hands and splashed cold water on their face, Nathan and Samuel loaded the sewing machine into the Zook's wagon.

As Abram dried his hands, his mind raced, thinking about how he could manage to sit near Sadie at the table. Since the family was eating outside, the seating would be more flexible.

"Sadie, do you need help?" Abram asked. "I can pull the pizzas out of the oven for you."

"I can manage," she replied with a smile. "Go ahead and sit."

Samuel took his seat at one of the corners of the table

and gestured to his children and guests to be seated as well. Sadie used the wooden paddles to remove the pizzas from the oven so that they could cool during their prayers. She was the last to be seated, and she glanced across the table to Abram and to her right to Nathan. Watching the young folks' jockeying for seating arrangements, Samuel smiled bowed his head to pray. The rest of the group followed his lead.

After a few moments of silence, Samuel cleared his throat, raised his eyes, and Sadie jumped up to slice and serve pizza. As Sadie brought plates to each person, Samuel noticed that Abram's eyes never left the girl. Deciding to shift some attention to his other guest, Samuel addressed Nathan.

"So off to college in the fall, are you, Nathan?" he asked. "Your parents will miss you, I'm sure."

"I won't be that far away," Nathan answered. "I'm going to Eastern Mennonite University in Virginia. I can come home on the weekends pretty often."

"Still, though, won't it be hard to be away from your family?" asked Sadie, finally sitting down to eat.

"I'm sure I'll miss them, but I'm excited about college. I'll meet so many new people."

"You'll probably forget about everyone here," Abram declared, gruffly.

Samuel watched Abram from the far end of the table. The boy seemed out of sorts, and Samuel wondered what troubled him. Sure, he was interested in Sadie, but he seemed upset by something.

"Well, no," Nathan said slowly. "I won't forget the

people I love here at home." Taking another bite of pizza, Nathan looked at Sadie. "Sadie, I don't think I could ever forget your cooking, not even if I lived on the other side of the world."

"Oh, Nathan, stop!" Sadie exclaimed. "Everyone helped. Cooking dinner is no reason to be proud. Everyone has to eat."

"It's not right to praise Plain folk for just doing their duty, Nathan. You should know that. Maybe Virginia is a better place for you," Abram said, his eyes focused on the boy across the table.

Samuel thought about intervening from the other end of the table, but decided to wait and see how Sadie handled herself. He wondered if there were a little rivalry between Nathan and Abram. He'd certainly never noticed it before, and he was sure that Sadie would never look at Nathan as a possible husband. They might believe many of the same things, but Plain living was very different from the way Nathan and his family lived.

"Good grief, man," Nathan exclaimed, as he leaned back from the table. "What's your deal? Did somebody make you an bishop and forget to notify the rest of us?"

"Do not make fun of our ways, Nathan Kobel," Abram warned. "We live the simple lives that God intended. We don't need your fancy schools and cars and…"

"Humility and plainness can mean letting others make their own decisions, Abram," Samuel interrupted from the far end of the table. "It is not for us to judge people who aren't Plain."

Feeling the truth and calm emanating from Samuel,

Abram bowed his head, sighed, and raised his eyes to Nathan's.

"I am sorry, Nathan. I spoke harshly and unfairly." Abram looked down at the table again and fell silent. Samuel's words had hurt him because he knew how very true they were. As conversation picked up around him – Miriam told a funny story about a student in school that day, and Isaac talked about the work he and young Samuel had done earlier – Abram was lost in his own thoughts.

He knew he had spoken out of frustration and anger, and he knew that he had been wrong to judge Nathan. But he also wondered if maybe he'd done the same thing to Sadie. Had he judged her too harshly as well? He knew that Plain people often examined each other's behavior and felt obligated to help each other behave properly, but he thought that he might have taken things a bit too far.

When Abram spent time with Sadie's family, he felt the warmth and the gentle support among the family members, and he realized just how differently his family worked. The Zook family felt nurturing while the Byler family felt harsher, more judgmental. Abram had really never thought about how different the two families were, and he thought that maybe he should try to be more understanding. Looking up from his dinner plate, Abram caught Sadie's eyes. He hoped that she would see the apology that his eyes held.

Abram caught back up with the discussion, and listened to Nathan explaining what he planned to study at school.

"One of the reasons I decided on EMU is the great education program. They also have a wonderful creative writing program, and I'm looking forward to taking some writing classes."

"Writing classes?" Sadie asked, excitedly. "What sort of things will you be writing?"

"Short stories, mostly, I expect. I'm not much for poetry, and I don't know that I have the patience for a novel."

Of course Sadie would be interested in Nathan's writing, Abram thought. Surely she wouldn't start making stories up! The journal was bad enough, but if she started writing stories? Abram frantically tried to come up with a way to shift the subject.

"So education? Are you thinking of being a teacher?" he asked.

"Maybe," Nathan answered. "Either a teacher or a writer."

Esther had been listening in from the other table, and she called out to Nathan, "Oh will you name a character in your book after me?"

"Well, Esther, I haven't even started a book yet, but I promise if I do that I'll name a character after you. She'll be a very smart and very good girl."

Miriam gently pointed out to Esther that she shouldn't be too proud or too interested in books about the English world.

"Will you write about Mennonites and Plain folk, Nathan?" Esther asked. "Or will you write about bad people?"

"I don't know, Esther. And not all English are bad. Some are good even though they don't live Plain."

But Da, if the English aren't bad, then why do we live separate from them?"

"Esther, that's a good question, and I think you know the answer already."

"I think it would be hard to follow the *ordnung* in the world," Esther said thoughtfully.

"That's right, Esther," Miriam said approvingly.

"And it's hard sometimes to follow God even if you're not Plain, being in the world," Nathan added. "It always helps me to remember that I want my parents to be proud of me, and that I shouldn't do anything that they would be ashamed of."

Sadie spoke up. "I'm sure your parents are pleased that you're going to school for education. Good teachers and good examples are so important for children."

"Where do you plan to teach?" Abram asked. "Maybe you could work in a missionary school in South America?"

Samuel laughed quietly and shook his head. He hoped that Abram didn't believe that he was being subtle.

"Maybe I will," Nathan answered. "I would like to travel and see more of the world."

Just as Abram seemed to relax a bit, Nathan gave him a sly glance and continued.

"But I'll always come back home to visit and to have some of Sadie's rhubarb pie."

Every person at the table except for Abram burst into laughter. He realized that his growing interest in Sadie wasn't quite as secret as he'd hoped, and now everyone thought he was ridiculous. Red-faced and muttering something about pie and pride, Abram stood and helped himself to another piece of pizza.

As dinner came to a close, Abram thought about the new journal Sadie had given him, and he wished that he could slip away and read it right away. He knew that he'd be expected to help the girls get the dishes inside, and he'd hoped for a chance to ask Sadie to go for a walk, but he thought he might better find a moment to talk to Nathan. The young men carried armloads of dishes into the kitchen, where the girls washed, dried, and put everything away.

While Samuel and Isaac banked the fire in the oven, Abram walked up to Nathan and offered his hand. As Nathan took it, Abram spoke.

"I am truly sorry, Nathan. I had no right to speak to you that way, and I had no right to judge you."

"No big deal, man," Nathan replied. "So does Sadie know that you're sweet on her?" he asked bluntly.

With a huge sigh, Abram shook his head and realized that there was no point in hiding his interest any longer.

"I don't think she even likes me, and I can't imagine that she's even noticed."

"You might be wrong about that, my man," Nathan replied, as he nodded in the direction of the house.

Abram turned to see Sadie looking directly at him through the kitchen window, a little smile on her face.

"I wonder if she'd agree to let me drive her home from

church on Sunday," Abram said, forgetting that Nathan was standing right next to him.

"There's only one way to find out," Nathan helpfully pointed out. "Sadie, I'm leaving," he called out toward the house. "Thanks for the wonderful dinner!"

Sadie stepped outside and waved at Nathan as he crossed the yard to his car. Young Samuel had harnessed a horse to the wagon and was ready to follow Nathan home with the sewing machine.

Sadie walked toward Abram, who stood uncomfortably fiddling with his hat that he hadn't yet put on following the meal.

"Will you be going too?" she asked Abram, looking up into his eyes.

"Yes. My father will need me to help him with a few things before it gets dark," he answered. "But there's something I want to ask you, Sadie."

"Yes?" she prompted.

"Will you sit with me at the ice cream social after church on Sunday?" Abram asked shyly, barely able to make eye contact.

"Of course," Sadie answered sweetly.

"And will you let me drive you home from church?"

"Of course. On one condition," she replied, with a smile and a bit of steel in her voice.

"Anything," Abram answered fervently.

"That you bring back both my journals. And I want you to answer what I wrote in the one I gave you tonight. Will you do that?"

"But Sadie, I'm no writer," Abram protested.

"That's not the point," Sadie insisted. "I want you to write something, anything, and I want you to give both of my books back."

Abram though for a moment and saw that he had no choice but to agree to her conditions.

"Okay, Sadie. You win. I'll see you Sunday."

As Abram swing himself up into his little courting buggy, he couldn't suppress a smile. He'd gotten Sadie to agree to let him drive her home! Even though Abram knew he shouldn't wish his life away, he wished that he didn't have to wait a whole day before he saw Sadie again.

Abram was exhausted by the time he arrived home, and he was thankful that his father and brothers had managed all the chores without him. He washed up before bed, and could hardly wait to crawl in bed with both of Sadie's books. He turned down the covers and reached beneath his pillow to retrieve her green journal, and he panicked when he touched nothing but the sheets beneath his pillow. Frantic, Abram threw the pillow aside, and saw the book on the far side of the bed, pushed way further than Abram recalled having left it.

Curious and concerned, Abram picked up the book, thumbed through it, and seeing nothing unusual, slowly set the book down. Worried that his mother may have found and read the book, Abram wasn't sure what to do. Figuring that his best bet was to act as if nothing had happened, Abram silently resolved to hide the books more carefully next time.

Settling into bed, Abram opened the little yellow book that Sadie had given him earlier that evening. It opened more stiffly, as it was a new book, with a single entry, dated that very day. Before he began reading, Abram let himself luxuriate in the thought of Sadie, curled up, bonnet removed, happily writing in the journal. He found himself thinking about how he might be able to see through the sheer organdy of her prayer cap. Stopping himself before his thoughts became impure, Abram returned his attention to the journal.

Abram started reading, and he was instantly transported to the day and scene that Sadie described. Even though he'd never participated in a quilting circle, he felt like he was there. When he got to the end of the passage, he was stunned by how simple, reverent, and sweet Sadie's story was. It was almost devotional, nearly a meditation. That Sadie could use a quilt square to teach Esther such an important lesson – and that she did it in such a loving and supportive way – made Abram realize that Sadie Zook was a very special girl.

When Abram read the words that Sadie had written to him, he was elated and humbled all at the same time. He reread the lines:

Abram, I thought of you after I wrote this passage, and I wanted you to read it. If you have thoughts on what I've written, I would welcome your response. You can write in this book and bring it to me when I see you next.

How could he have been so foolish and so proud to think that he knew better than Sadie what was right for her? He held in his hands a book written by a young woman who was a model for other Plain young women.

She was good, wholesome, humble, and using the talents that God had given her. Glad that he had thought to bring a pencil upstairs, Abram ran his fingers over the words that Sadie had written just a few hours ago.

He collected his thoughts and began to write.

Chapter Eight

Saturday dawned gray and chilly. As Abram rose early and joined his father and younger brothers in the barn to begin their chores, he was determined to get through the day without mooning over Sadie like a silly little boy. He and Luke Stoltzfos had agreed to ride together to Bishop King's farm and get the church wagon with the backless benches that were moved to the hosting family's house for church services. The wagon was immense, and the drive would take nearly two hours. Abram found that he was pleased at the prospect of some quiet time to himself.

Finishing his chores and breakfast, Abram concealed Sadie's two journals beneath his jacket and headed out to hitch his horse to the buggy for the ride to the Stoltzfos farm. Carefully sliding the journals into the compartment beneath the little buggy's seat, Abram started the short drive to Luke's farm. Hoping the day would warm up a little and that the rain would hold off until after he and Luke had gotten the wagon back and the benches unloaded, the mile between the Byler and Stoltzfos houses went quickly.

Pulling into the yard, Abram was surprised and suddenly flushed when he saw one of the Zook's buggies already there. Abram was so excited by the possibility of seeing Sadie that he nearly forgot to tie his horse up at the barn. He hurried toward the house, hoping for a glimpse of the girl who so occupied his thoughts.

As he approached the house, Luke opened the door before Abram could even knock. Luke was happily watching his mother and Miriam Zook working together to make enough pies to feed the crowd of people who would fill the house on Sunday. Distracting Miriam with a wink, Luke swiped a strawberry from the bowl Miriam stirred, and turned to Abram.

"Ready to go?" he asked.

"Sure," Abram answered. "Miriam, did Sadie come with you?" he asked.

"No, she's home taking care of Mama and cleaning house with Esther. Why?"

"Oh nothing important," Abram answered hurriedly, attempting to conceal his disappointment. "Let's get going before the rain starts."

The two young men climbed into Abram's buggy and set off for Elder King's farm. As they made the three-mile journey to the farm, Abram talked about crops and business, and Luke talked about Miriam. Abram was curious about how the two of them had gotten together – how they'd managed to make the move from acquaintances to sweethearts. He couldn't figure out how to ask without prying or arousing Luke's suspicions. Believing that he still had a chance to keep his interest in Sadie a secret, Abram decided to stay quiet and learn as much as he could from Luke's ceaseless talk of Miriam.

When they arrived at Bishop King's house, they pulled up next to the massive church wagon. Something like a trailer-wagon hybrid, the wagon held the benches that would crowd the Stoltzfos' living room and hold the entire congregation for worship services. With an anxious eye on the gathering clouds on the horizon, the boys hitched horses to the wagon, bid goodbye to Bishop King, and set off.

Happy to arrive back to the farm just as the first raindrops hit the ground, Abram promised to arrive a few minutes early the next morning to help Luke and his father unload the heavy benches and get them set up in inside. Abram found that he'd never looked forward to a Sunday as much as he did this one. He knew full well that Sadie's promise to let him drive her home and to sit with him at the ice cream social after services had everything to do with his anticipation.

❦ ❦ ❦

Sadie awoke early and smiled as she thought about the dream that her alarm clock had interrupted. Thinking about the smell of wood shavings and a tall, broad-shouldered young man with brown hair, Sadie hummed to herself as she made her bed and dressed in her newest dark purple dress. She always wore her newest dress to church, not because she was proud, but because it showed a respect and reverence for God.

She brushed her long blonde hair, freshly washed from the night before, and she carefully braided it and wound it neatly into a bun that she covered with her prayer covering. She pinned the stiff white damask covering in place, lifted her clean black bonnet from its place on a peg, and she headed downstairs to start breakfast.

Pleasantly surprised to see her mother up and about, Sadie inquired after Hannah's health.

"I'm feeling much better, Sadie. I think I'll even be able to go to church this morning."

"Miriam and I will make sure Esther is ready, and we will make sure the dishes are washed too. You can sit and rest, Mama."

Smiling her thanks, Hannah turned some sausages that sizzled on the stove, and waved Sadie over to crack and scramble the eggs. Joined by Miriam and Hannah, the ladies had breakfast ready just as the men finished up the outside chores.

"Looks like the sun will shine today," Samuel observed as he dried his hands. "We'll be eating ice cream this afternoon, for sure," he predicted.

"I hope so, Da," Esther exclaimed! "Miriam let me put the chocolate chips in our ice cream, and it will be the most delicious you have ever tasted!"

"Now, Esther," Hannah said in her sweet, but firm tone. "We aren't proud and boastful. We do not compete among ourselves over ice cream, or anything else."

Hannah passed the sausage to her youngest daughter and added, "I bet your ice cream will be delicious, though."

"Miriam, I assume that you will find a ride home from church this afternoon?" Samuel asked.

"Yes, Da," Miriam answered primly, choosing to say nothing further.

"And you Sadie?" Samuel asked. "Will you be riding home with us or will you find your own way home?"

"I have also made arrangements for a ride home, Da."

Sadie smiled to herself at the breakfast table before she realized that every member of her family was watching to see if she planned to elaborate. Since it wasn't unusual for a young lady to keep her own counsel when she began seeing a new young man. Sadie looked around the table, gave a little shrug, and poured herself a glass of milk.

After breakfast, Sadie took Esther upstairs to help her get ready for church. While Sadie brushed Esther's long hair that was just a slightly darker shade of honey than Sadie's own, the girls talked about how they both looked forward to eating ice cream after lunch.

"I won't even tell my friends which ice cream is ours," Esther declared. "But I bet it will be the first one gone!"

Shaking her head at the young girl's enthusiasm, Sadie didn't say a word.

"So who are you riding home from church with, Sadie? Is it Abram Byler?" Esther asked with a sly grin.

"Why, what on earth would make you ask that, Esther?" sputtered Sadie.

"Everyone can tell that he likes you."

Sadie just stared at Esther and couldn't think of a

thing to say. She braided her sister's hair, wound it up into a bun, and pinned her prayer cap in place. Esther grabbed her black bonnet and skipped out the door, while Sadie sat and thought for a moment.

How could everyone know that Abram liked her? Their first full conversation with him had just happened a few short days ago. And that hadn't even been a very friendly conversation! As she smoothed her dress and apron, Sadie realized how much she was hoping that Abram had taken the time to answer her journal entry. Even if he'd only written a few words, Sadie wanted to continue their conversation.

The Zook family piled into two buggies – young Samuel and Isaac rode together in Samuel's two-seater, and Samuel, Hannah, Miriam, Sadie, and Esther climbed into the larger buggy. As they set off on the drive to the farm, both Sadie and Miriam were anxious to arrive.

When the Zooks arrived at the Stoltzfos farm, there was a line of buggies in the road, waiting to turn in to the drive. The Stoltzfos boys were on hand to direct buggies coming in and to help unhitch and water the horses. Ladies brought in dishes piled high with food for the lunch the congregation would share after their worship. Children ran to greet one another, and as soon as Esther had helped a basket of food inside, she vanished to play for a few minutes while the rest of the families arrived.

The Stoltzfos family's living room was crowded, the large rectangular room full to the edges with benches, divided down the middle by an open aisle. As church members greeted one another warmly, people began to filter into the living room to get ready for the service. Women sat on one side of the aisle, and the men on the other side.

Sadie was glad that this week's service was at the Stoltzfos farm. When the house had been built, the living room had been designed with the entire congregation of twenty or so families in mind. In some of the smaller houses of the community, the members filled up several rooms, and Sadie always found it harder to pay attention if they were spread out and she couldn't see the preacher.

The process of getting every member inside always took some time, but it was one of Sadie's favorite parts of the day. Sadie hadn't yet been baptized, but she would begin her instruction in two weeks when the church service would be at the Zook's house. She looked forward to the services after her baptism when she, as a full adult member of the congregation, would greet all of her sisters with a holy kiss.

Sadie watched Miriam kiss each of the baptized women, and she reflected on how simple and sweet the ritual was. As most Plain folk weren't showy or public in expressions of affection, Sadie thought the practice of taking a moment to greet every one of your sisters with an expression of love was beautiful. She had noticed, though, that not all of the women seemed to enjoy the holy kiss, and they seemed awkward and embarrassed. Sister King smacked each woman soundly on the lips and welcomed each member with a smile. Ruth Byler was the opposite, and Sadie noticed the disapproving set of her mouth and chaste peck that barely lasted a split second.

Hannah had waved off her sisters' kisses, as she'd been sick and didn't want to spread her illness, so she and Sadie sat down together before most of the women had finished greeting one another. Sadie enjoyed sitting quietly and watching the members of the congregation greet one another and begin to settle in for the service. Miriam joined her mother and sister and waved at Esther sitting with one of her friends.

The men began to filter into the room, and Sadie couldn't help but focus on Abram. Taller than most of the men in the room, he carried himself with a rigid, upright stance that made him stand out even more. She watched as he greeted the preacher in the center of the room with a kiss, and Sadie found herself utterly lost in thought. She stared at Abram's mouth and imagined what it would be like to kiss him. She imagined a quiet moment with just the two of them and a single chaste kiss.

Sadie came to her senses with Miriam's elbow in her ribs. Though she tried to hide her smile behind a stern expression, Miriam couldn't quite keep her amusement to herself.

"You're staring," she whispered. "People will notice."

A little embarrassed, Sadie saw that someone had indeed noticed when she felt Ruth Byler's eyes on her. Modestly bowing her head and folding her hands in her lap, Sadie calmed her thoughts and brought them back to the church service that was about to begin. The sermon and the singing always made Sadie feel like a part of a huge family.

When the last hymn was sung, the women headed

to the kitchen to get lunch ready. Since the day was clear and warm, the entire congregation would be able to eat all together, as the Kings had more than a dozen picnic tables outside under the large shade trees. Sadie always enjoyed the meals at which everyone could be seated together. Had the day been rainy, the men would have eaten first at the tables inside, and the women would have been seated afterwards.

Young children played and helped set the tables, while the young women began to carry out platters of food. Fresh baked rolls, ham, potato salad, roast beef, and vegetables filled the tables, and once most of the group was seated, Sadie and a few of the other young women poured coffee and ice water for the congregation.

Sadie discreetly kept her eye on Abram, though he was seated at a table far from the one at which she was pouring coffee. Noticing her attention, he rewarded her with a shy little smile, and just a hint of a blush in his cheeks.

Miriam watched the interplay from her seat next to Hannah, and she noticed that the eye contact between Abram and Sadie did not go unremarked. Abram's attention was drawn away from Sadie by a stern word from Ruth Byler, and Sadie returned her focus to the empty glasses in front of her.

Glasses filled and everyone seated, Bishop King bowed his head and the rest of the congregation followed suit. After a few moments of silence, he cleared his throat to signal the end of the silent prayers. Forks and knives clattered as hungry worshipers filled their plates and began to share in the meal. The conversation was quiet, and Sadie noticed Abram stealing glances at her from time to time. She also noticed that Jacob Stoltzfos was trying to catch her eye as well. He was such a nice fellow – smart, funny, and a hard worker – but Sadie couldn't find it in her to like him as anything more than a friend. She was pretty certain that he'd ask to drive her home later, and she worked on a polite way to decline his offer.

As lunch wound down, the women started to clear and wash dishes, and the young men started to put up the volleyball net. Since there was still time to play before the ice cream needed to be set up, Sadie and Miriam hurried outside to join in the fun. Both girls knew that when they married and had children of their own that the days of carefree play would be over, so they resolved to enjoy it while it lasted.

"Sadie! There you are!" shouted Jacob Stoltzfos. Dashing up to her and grabbing her elbow, Jacob was clearly happy to see her.

"Jacob. How are you?"

"I'll be happy if you agree to let me drive you home this afternoon," Jacob said, leaning toward her.

Taking a step back, Sadie shook her head.

"I can't Jacob. I've already promised someone else."

"What? Who?" Jacob demanded loudly, still gripping her elbow.

"Well since you asked, it's Abram Byler," Sadie answered, trying to pull her arm from his grasp.

"Abram Byler, that old man?" Jacob scoffed. "You won't have any fun with him."

"Well I plan to let him drive me home nonetheless," Sadie replied. "Let's go play some volleyball," she continued, hoping to change the subject.

"Well all right," Jacob agreed, in a sulky tone. "But you have to be on my team"

"Sure, Jacob," Sadie answereTurning to walk to the volleyball game, Sadie noticed Abram watching her talk to Jacob, and he looked none too happy. Teams were sorted out to be relatively evenly matched, and despite Abram's not-so-subtle attempt to be on Sadie's team, he was stuck on the other side because he and Jacob Stoltzfos were the tallest. Despite Abram's height, he wasn't the best player. Miriam Zook was surprisingly good, with a serve that always seemed to find the weakest player.

Though the games weren't suppose to be competitive, cheers and encouragement were commonplace, and Jacob, in particular, seemed to delight in Abram's shortcoming. The biggest smile Sadie had seen on Abram's face all day – perhaps ever – came when Abram blocked a shot of Jacob's and won the point for his team. Sadie's team rallied, though and won the game.

Hot and sweaty, the volleyball players were thrilled when they saw the women bringing ice cream and bowls outside. Abram sought out Sadie's eyes, as if he wanted to remind her that she'd promised to sit with him. She shyly smiled at him, and the pair walked over to get ice cream. Abram led Sadie to a table not yet occupied, and they sat at the far end, so they might have a few moments to themselves.

"Sadie," Abram said softly. "You will let me drive you home today?"

"That depends, Abram," Sadie replied, with a little smile.

"Depends? But you said on Friday that you would let me drive you home," Abram hotly protested.

"It depends on whether you brought my books."

"Oh," Abram sighed. "I did bring them. They're in my buggy."

"And did you write to me?" Sadie asked quietly.

"I did."

"Oh, Abram, I can't wait to read it," Sadie whispered as she leaned closer to the young man.

Before Abram could reply, his sister, Katie, skipped over and stood right behind the pair. Abram and Sadie turned to face her, and Katie smiled brightly.

"Abram, Mama told me to come sit with you. She said you wouldn't mind scooting over so that I can sit between you and Sadie."

Abram looked over toward the house and saw Ruth, stern-faced and glaring at him. She turned on her heel and walked back indoors as Katie settled down and started in on her strawberry ice cream.

Katie chattered gaily between spoonfuls of ice cream. "I love ice cream, and I wish we could have it more often. Mama says that too many conveniences will make us too worldly, though. I think a freezer would be okay. What do you think Abram?"

"I'm sure that Mother and Father are right, Katie," he answered distractedly.

"But you have a freezer, right, Sadie?" Katie asked, turning to the older girl.

"We do, Katie, you're right."

"Does that make you worldly?"

"Katie, we are Plain, same as you."

"But why does Mama say that a freezer is worldly, then?" Katie asked her brother.

"That's enough, Katie. The Zooks follow the *ordnung*, and so do we. If you have more questions, you should ask Father and Mother."

"Okay, Abram," the girl replied. "I just love ice cream, and I wish we could have it at home more often."

"I understand," Abram said thoughtfully. "I understand completely."

After all of the ice cream had been devoured, and after all of the dishes had been cleaned up, families began to pack up the buggies to return home. Luke Stoltzfos and Abram loaded all of the benches into the church wagon so that Bishop King could drive the wagon back to his house until it was needed for the Zooks' house in two weeks.

Abram looked at Sadie as he hitched his horse to his buggy. She stood near the house, talking and laughing with some of the women who were helping rinse out and pack up the water glasses they'd used for lunch. Sadie was so warm and generous with her smiles and laughter, and Abram wondered, in a moment of insecurity, if she'd only agreed to ride home with him because she wanted her journals back. As he caught Sadie's eye, though, he realized that he was being silly. He might have her journals, but she had written lines meant just for him.

Having readied his buggy for the trip to the Zook's, Abram approached John Byler. "Father, I'm driving Sadie Zook home today. I'll be home later, in time for chores."

John Byler looked at his son, nodded, and stiffly replied, "See that you are home on time, Abram."

Sadie took her leave of her friends, and with a wave to Hannah, joined Abram at his buggy.

"Ready?" Abram asked, as he offered his hand to help Sadie into the buggy.

"Absolutely," Sadie answered.

As Abram's courting buggy pulled away from the Stoltzfos farm, Ruth Byler came outside to look for her husband. As she caught sight of a bonnet in her son's buggy, she hurried to John.

'Who is that in Abram's buggy?" she demanded.

"It is Sadie Zook," John answered.

"Did you know the Abram planned to drive her home? Did he tell you?"

"Ruth, what does it matter? The boy is old enough to make his own decisions. He'll be a man married soon enough."

Ruth looked at John with shock. "You would let him ride around with a worldly girl in his buggy for all the world to see?

"Ruth, that's Sadie Zook. She's a good, steady girl. He could do worse."

"John, she has you fooled. You and Abram both."

John watched Ruth's back as she stormed away.

Puzzled, as he'd never known a member of the Zook household to be accused of wickedness, he wondered what his wife was so upset about. The Zooks were certainly less strict about some aspects of the *ordnung* than the Bylers were, but John had no idea what Ruth was talking about. He was certain that she'd give him an earful later.

Chapter Nine

A few minutes passed before Sadie broke the silence that built in the little buggy.

"So," she began. "Can I read what you wrote?"

"Not while I'm sitting here!" Abram exclaimed, as if the thought of sitting and waiting for Sadie to read his entry positively horrified him. "Will you wait until you're alone?"

"I suppose so," Sadie answered.

"It's just that you're so good at writing, and I am, well, not very good at it."

Looking sideways at Abram, Sadie smiled. "You think I'm good at writing?" she asked softly.

"Of course I do," Abram answered. "When I'm reading your journal, I feel like I'm right there. I've had to stop myself from laughing out loud at some of your stories so my family won't hear me and wonder what is going on."

"You've laughed at my stories?" Sadie asked, with wonder in her voice.

"Well, of course."

Facing the front and leaning back against the buggy's seat, Sadie was quiet and thoughtful. It had never occurred to her that other people might like to read what she had written. The thought of Abram Byler reading her journal and laughing – not because he thought it was silly, but because he liked it – was so strange. She worried for a moment about how she felt. She realized that it would be far too easy to feel proud of her writing, and that would do nothing but prove that she had sinned by keeping a journal.

"That was never my intention," Sadie said firmly. "You must know that. I didn't want you to read my book, and you should have just given it back to me."

"Wait a minute, Sadie," Abram said urgently, placing his hand over hers. "I have to explain something to you." Abram paused and thought for a moment to make sure that his words came out the way he wanted them to. "When I first found your journal, I was sure that it was sinful for you to have written it. I thought you were being selfish and proud."

Seeing Sadie slouch a little, as if she were dejected, Abram squeezed her hand lightly and continued. "I thought it was sinful, but I was wrong. Sadie, I was completely wrong."

Sadie turned to Abram, and he was surprised to see tears sparkling on her eyelashes.

"You were wrong?"

"I was wrong, Sadie. I realized that you do write about the English world, but it's not because you want to live in it. You write about Nathan Kobel, but not because you want to be like him. You write about the things that are important to you, and your journal shows the heart of a humble, Plain woman who I admire.

"Sadie, I was wrong, and you were right. I ask for your forgiveness. I should not have judged you so unfairly."

Eyes shining, Sadie looked at Abram, simply speechless. She couldn't believe that Abram had just spoken those words to her. Abram Byler, grouchy, rigid Abram Byler not only thought that she was a good writer, but he had also apologized to her.

Realizing that Sadie wasn't going to speak right away, Abram decided to continue. "Sadie, when I read your story about Esther's quilt, I understood. Your writing is like a prayer. You connect your life with your faith in a way that is simple and honest."

"You understand," Sadie whispered, in awe.

"I do," Abram replied. "I do understand. I'm giving your books back, and I would like it if you would write more and let me read it. I promise to keep your secret, and I feel honored that I get to share it with you."

Sadie smiled and turned her hand underneath Abram's so that her palm met his. Holding still and feeling the warmth of his hand, Sadie felt a thrill of sheer happiness. Looking sideways at him again, with a half smile and peering through her lashes, Sadie told Abram that she looked forward to reading his entry in her journal.

"Please don't judge me too harshly," he replied with a rueful smile. "You know I'm no fancy college boy, and I don't have the natural talent that God gave you."

"As long as you are honest and open, then I am

certain that what you write will be worth reading," Sadie answered.

The two young people sat in silence for nearly a mile. Both were aware of their hands touching. Sadie liked that Abram's hand rested lightly on hers. She enjoyed the feeling of contact without pressure. Abram was thrilled to feel Sadie's small hand beneath his, but the longer he thought about it, the harder it became to keep his head from straying into subjects that weren't proper.

Abram cleared his throat and put both hands on the reins as he sat up a little straighter. He surely didn't want to make Sadie feel uncomfortable. In fact, he was hoping that she would feel comfortable enough to consider letting him drive her home from church a second time. He knew that he had to exercise restraint and behave properly.

"Do you have a safe place to keep your books at home?" asked Abram, in an attempt to take his mind away from Sadie's soft skin.

"I do," she answered. "I keep my journals under my pillow when they're at home, and I keep them tucked away among the files at work." Sadie thought for a second. "You kept the books hidden, right? I don't want your mother to find them. I don't want to have to explain myself to the whole congregation," she continued, with alarm in her voice.

"I'm pretty sure the books have been safe," Abram answered, hoping that he was right. "I kept them under my pillow as well."

Sadie blushed bright red as she thought about Abram

reading her books in bed, and she abruptly changed the subject.

"I don't think Jacob Stoltzfos was very happy with you today. He had a mind to drive me home again."

"I'm surely glad that I asked you before he did," Abram said with a smile.

"As am I," Sadie agreed.

Abram and Sadie talked companionably, and despite Abram's deliberate and subtle attempt to slow his horse's progress, before the pair knew it, they'd arrived at the Zook's home. Sadie realized that she had enjoyed every minute of the ride, and she hoped for Abram to ask to drive her home again.

Wishing he could prolong their afternoon, Abram knew that he needed to get home to help his father with chores before it got too late. He looked at the lovely girl next to him and quietly addressed her. "Will you write some more in the journal and bring it to work tomorrow?" he asked, discovering that he could hardly wait to see Sadie again.

"Yes, I will, Abram. And I thank you for the lovely drive home and for your kind words," Sadie answered, with a touch of shyness that was quite unlike her.

"I will look forward to reading what you write. And perhaps we could go for a drive again?" he asked hopefully.

"I'd like that very much," Sadie said with a broad smile.

Abram pulled on the reins to stop the horse, and he reached into the compartment beneath his seat to retrieve her journals. Before he surrendered the books, he ran his fingers along the edges, much as he'd done the very first time he saw the little green book. Without a word, Abram placed the books in Sadie's hands, and he watched as she carefully slid the books beneath her apron. Abram helped Sadie out of the buggy, and he watched her walk inside. As she reached the kitchen door, she turned, smiled, and waved to the young man whose smile matched her own.

When Sadie walked through the kitchen door, she found Miriam waiting, with an inquisitive look in her eye.

"Drive okay?" her sister asked, as if the question were a common one.

"Fine, thank you," Sadie answered. "Actually it was quite nice. Surprisingly nice," Sadie finished, with a hint of wonder in her voice. "I'll be in my room if anyone needs me. I'm a little tired, and I'd like to lay down for a bit."

As Miriam watched her sister leave the room, she remembered the very first time that Luke had driven her home, and how much she'd enjoyed his company. Miriam hoped that Sadie would be as lucky in finding a man to marry.

Sadie walked up the steps, into her room, and she closed the door. She felt a bit dazed by the afternoon, and she was happy to have a few moments to herself to think everything through. Withdrawing her journals from beneath her apron, she opened the little yellow book and turned to the single page that was written with a masculine hand.

Sadie, I feel like a fool. Your journals have been a gift from God to me. I know that I'm awkward, and I'm not good with words like you and like Nathan Kobel, but I see more than just your words. Your writing — the writing you do with the gifts God has given you —has helped me realize one of the most important things the Plain people believe. Lessons in humility are everywhere. God's path is clear if we take the time to look for it.

You reminded me of that, and I thank you. If you will write to me, I will read your words, and I will keep your secret. I will keep your secret because I believe that you are using the talents God gave you.

I look forward to reading more.

Yours,
Abram

Sadie closed the book and held it to her chest. She never would have guessed that stern Abram Byler could understand he as well as he clearly did. She never would have expected that a man who could hardly speak a single sentence without sounding like an angry old man could actually write something so sweet. As Sadie held her journal, she thought about how precious this newfound connection with Abram was to her. She found that she not only looked forward to seeing him on Monday, but she also wanted to write to him and read his response.

She found that she actually cared about what he would say.

Reaching for the pen that Sadie kept in her the drawer of her bedside table, Sadie opened her yellow journal and began to write.

"For there is nothing hid, which shall not be manifested; neither was any thing kept secret, but that it should come abroad."

Mark 4:22

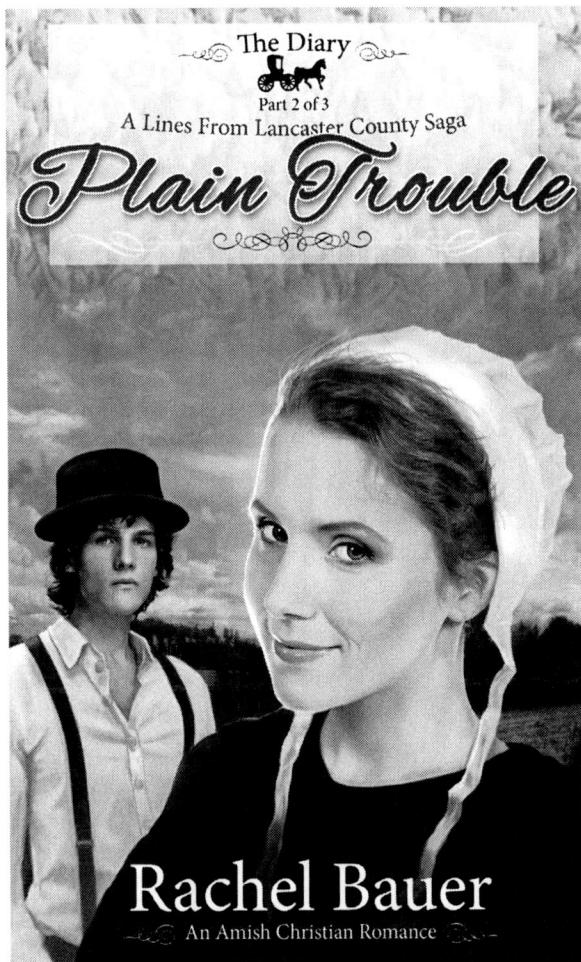

The Diary

Part 2 of 3

A Lines From Lancaster County Saga

Plain Trouble

Rachel Bauer

An Amish Christian Romance

Chapter Ten

Even before his alarm went off at 5 am, Abram Byler was wide awake. He lay in his bed watching the hands on his wind-up alarm clock, and he wondered why time seemed to crawl. Slipping his hand beneath his pillow, he felt the coarse fabric cover of the journal he had hidden there the night before. Since he still had several minutes before he was expected in the barn to help with the morning chores, Abram decided to indulge himself in the luxury of rereading the most recent entry in the journal.

Abram lit the oil lamp on the nightstand and opened the yellow journal to the pages he'd read the night before.

It seems so strange to be writing and knowing that someone – that you – will be reading it. For so long, my journals have been my secret, and now you share that secret, Abram.

At work today, I met the most interesting customers. I thought about you when the two men came into

*the store, and while I answered their questions and
helped them with the order for a dining table and
chairs, I wondered what you would think of them.
When they first walked in, I didn't realize that there
was anything unusual about them, but when it
became clear that they were picking out furniture for
the house they lived in together, I realized that they
were gay. I had never met a gay person before, at
least not anyone I knew was gay.*

*I think they could tell the moment that I knew, and
I think they were a little worried that I would either
refuse to deal with them, or that I might be rude to
them. It was hard to tell what they were thinking,
but I paused for a moment and decided that they
deserved the same courtesy that all of our customers
do. They seemed a little relieved when I sat down
with them to write up their order.*

*I had so many thoughts running through my head
while they were in the store, and one of them – his
name was Jack – was really funny and charming.
I know that being gay is sinful, and I wouldn't
want any of my brothers to live that way. I thought
to myself, though, that these men were someone's
sons and brothers, and they deserve to be treated
with respect. I wondered if you would feel any
differently, and I wondered if you would have felt
uncomfortable.*

*As they were leaving, Nathan Kobel pulled into the
yard, and he came inside to see me. His mother had*

*embroidered some dishtowels for Mama to thank
her for the loan of her sewing machine a couple of
weeks ago. The needlework on the towels is really
lovely, and they're really too pretty to use, but we'll
use them anyway.*

*Nathan said he'd noticed your buggy at our house a
few times recently, and he asked if you and I might
like to go with him to Speedwell Forge Lake over near
Lititz on Friday evening. It's about fifteen miles away,
but Nathan offered to drive. He's going to take a girl
named Meredith from his school, and he thought
we could have a picnic. He said he wasn't sure if you
would want to go, but he thought it would be fun.
He said he could pick us up at my house on Friday
around six. I told him I'd ask you and let him know
tomorrow if he could stop in the store.*

*It was an interesting day at work. What do you think
about Friday?*

Abram smiled to himself, still hardly able to believe
that in just a couple of weeks, his whole world had
changed. It seemed like a lifetime ago that he'd discovered
Sadie Zook's journal in a box of files, and since that day,
nothing had been the same. Though he'd initially been
horrified at the notion of Sadie's secret writing, he had
come to realize that her writing wasn't a sin, and in fact
was a spiritual, devotional record of the devout young
woman's life. Not only had Abram and Sadie reached an
understanding about her journals, but they'd also begun

a new and exciting relationship. Abram had never felt quite so alive.

Abram's eyes fell back to the journal, and he reread what he'd written to Sadie the night before. Satisfied with his words, Abram closed the book and decided that it was close enough to 5am to get his day started. He put on his black pants with suspenders, light blue shirt, and he lifted his straw hat from its peg on the bedroom wall.

Tucking Sadie's journal into the back of his pants, Abram headed downstairs to the kitchen. Hoping to make it outside before anyone else in the house was up, he slipped through the downstairs rooms without lighting any of the lamps. Relieved to be outside, Abram took a deep breath of the cool June morning air. He hurried to the barn, intent on hiding Sadie's journal in his buggy before anyone else could see it.

Even though he didn't think the Sadie was sinning in her writing, he knew for sure that some members of his family and of their congregation would disagree. Abram had noticed that his mother had been keeping a closer eye on him than usual, and he suspected that she might have read one of the journals. He hadn't mentioned his suspicions to Sadie, and he certainly hadn't brought the matter up with his stern mother.

As Abram safely stowed Sadie's journal, he reflected that he felt a little smothered by his mother's eagle eye and the attention from both of his parents that felt a little oppressive at times. He hadn't realized just how different and how strict his parents were until he'd spent a little time at the Zook's house.

The congregation that the Bylers and the Zooks belonged to was average in size for Plain folk, and there was a range of attitudes toward technology and its place in a Plain household. The Zooks, for example, had two generators for their house, and they had a refrigerator and electric lights in some of the rooms of their home. John and Ruth Byler, though, had always taken a less permissive path. While there was a generator in the barn that could have been used to fuel some appliances that would make life easier for the Byler family, they chose to live with even fewer modern comforts than many of the members of their congregation.

Abram hadn't ever really questioned his parents and their rules, but having seen that Sadie and her family had a few conveniences and still managed to live Plain and devout, Abram found that he was having trouble making sense of it all. He was surprised to discover that he felt a little resentment at his mother's disapproving glances, especially because he felt in his heart that his conscience was clear. Silently resolving to stand up for himself a bit more – after all, he was twenty-one years old – Abram got to work on his chores.

Joined by his father and by his younger brothers Joshua and little John, together they fed and watered their livestock, milked the two cows, picked some fresh strawberries, and did some weeding in the huge garden near the barn. By the time the breakfast bell rang, the men were finished with their work and hungry for breakfast.

Little John ran ahead and burst through the kitchen door with his basket of strawberries. As he rushed to place the strawberries in the sink and get some breakfast, he slipped on some water on the floor and just barely managed to catch himself on the edge of the counter.

"Oh hell!" Little John blurted, as he scrambled to catch the strawberries that had spilled out of the basket.

"John Byler, you will not use such language in this house, and you will not sit at this table if you talk that way," Ruth scolded. "Do you learn such language from the boys at work?"

"Sorry, Mother," Little John replied, still picking strawberries up off the floor. "It won't happen again."

"See, John," Ruth snapped at her husband. "This is what happens when they mix with people who are worldly. He learns vulgar words from those boys at the Stoltzfos farm."

"John, take your breakfast outside and eat at the table by yourself," John told his youngest son. "We will not have such awful language in this house."

Eleven-year-old Katie helped her big brother pick up the remaining berries, while twenty-two-year-old Sarah fixed a plate for Little John. Abram silently washed his hands and thought about what had just happened. He knew that Little John shouldn't have used a curse word, especially in front of Katie, but he also couldn't help feeling a little envious of John, as he got to eat outside, separate from the kitchen's stifling climate.

Abram and his family sat down to breakfast, and Ruth glared at the empty chair where her youngest son would have been. John bowed his head, and the family followed suit, each member praying silently. Abram thought about how different meals were with his family compared to Sadie's family. The Byler table was usually quiet, except for the sounds of forks on plates and occasional requests for a dish to be passed.

John and Ruth had raised their children very strictly, and while the Zooks enjoyed lively conversation at their table, the Bylers engaged in very little idle conversation. Ruth and John squelched frivolous conversation with Bible verses wielded like weapons. Abram was certain that he could recite from memory every single verse in the entirety of the Scriptures that dealt with idle talk. Matthew 12:36 was one of Ruth's favorites: "But I say unto you, That every idle word that men shall speak, they shall give account thereof in the day of judgment."

Abram had always accepted his parents' teachings, but he wondered now. Were the Zooks less righteous? Were they worldly and less Plain just because they laughed and talked during family meals? Abram wondered if perhaps matters weren't as black and white as his parents had always taught.

Deciding to test the waters a bit, Abram boldly spoke up. "Father, do you have Samuel Zook's paperwork ready for me to take in? I can do it today if you'd like."

John nodded at Abram without saying a word and turned his attention back to his plate. Abram looked around the table and settled his gaze on Sarah. He decided to push a little harder to start conversation.

"Sarah, I suppose the market will be busy today Saturday since it's supposed to be a nice weekend?" he asked.

Sarah looked startled at the unusual breakfast conversation. She warily glanced down the table at her mother and chose to answer her brother. "Yes, Abram, I expect we will be busy."

Ruth cleared her throat without ever removing her eyes from her breakfast. Abram knew that his attempts to start conversation were unusual and likely to result in some conflict, but he felt strangely compelled to stir things up in a way he never had before. He pressed on in his attempt to draw Sarah into talking about the market where she worked, selling produce and baked goods.

"There will be lots of Englishers out this weekend, here to stare at the Plain people," Abram continued. "Sadie says that it's almost funny to watch them, so awkward…" Abram's voice trailed off as his mother's eyes had locked on his as soon as he'd spoken Sadie's name. He felt a tangible emotion from her seat at the table, and he was so startled by her immediate and intense reaction that he stopped speaking.

"Abram, we will not spend another second talking about the English and people who are so proud that they think they can mix with them," Ruth said quietly, but with venom in her voice.

"But, Mother," Abram started.

"Abram, no," John said flatly. "You will obey your mother."

Abram slumped in his chair a bit, feeling deflated by the way in which his parents had shut down his attempt at conversation. The rest of the meal passed in silence. After breakfast, the family members prepared to go their separate ways. John would retreat to his home office to do his accounting work – primarily for other Plain families in the area. Sarah would help Ruth with the dishes and a few more chores before leaving for her job at the Amish Market in a few hours. Abram would head to Ephrata Woodworks, where he would see Sadie and her father, Samuel. Eighteen-year-old Joshua worked with Bishop King at his farm, and John would head to the Stoltzfos Dairy – a huge operation that also employed two of Sadie Zook's brothers.

As Abram finished his preparations to leave for work, he thought about his mother's reaction to Sadie's name. He remembered the evening, shortly after having found Sadie's journal, when he had discovered the little cloth-covered book not exactly where he had left it. He'd wondered for a couple of weeks if perhaps his mother had found and read the journal; he was now pretty sure she had.

Shrugging into his black jacket, Abram addressed his parents. "I will be home late this evening. I have plans after work." Before either of his parents could say a word, Abram was out the door, headed for the barn. He hitched his horse to his buggy, and he left for work.

Back inside, Ruth turned to her husband. "He'll probably be spending time with that Sadie Zook," she muttered.

"Ruth, what is wrong with Sadie?" John asked. "Samuel and Hannah have been friends and Samuel has been a customer for many years."

"They set a bad example with their electricity at home, and they have a telephone at their store, and that Sadie!

Did you hear Abram mention that Sadie is always talking about the English. She'll end up leaving, that girl will."

"Ruth, we live a little more simply than the Zooks, but that doesn't mean they're proud. They are still Plain, and Sadie is young. You know, it wasn't that long ago that I remember another girl that some in the congregation thought might leave," John said quietly.

"John Byler, how dare you?" Ruth whispered angrily. "You promised me that we would never talk of that again. And you should talk! Your family isn't so pure, if I remember correctly!"

Ruth spun on her heel and left the kitchen. In her wake she left her husband, shaking his head, and her children, faces betraying their curiosity at their parents' whispered and heated exchange.

Chapter Eleven

Sadie whistled one of her favorite hymns as she packed the lunch she would take to work for her father, Abram, and herself. Adding a few fresh baked brownies to the top of the basket she used each day, Sadie knew exactly why she was in such good spirits. In an hour or so, she would see Abram at work, and she hoped that she would be spending that evening with him, Nathan Kobel, and Meredith. Sadie didn't know Meredith well, but she did know that Meredith wasn't a Mennonite like Nathan. She found that she was both curious and apprehensive about spending the evening with the girl, not knowing a thing about her.

The last couple of weeks had been at once vexing and exciting as she and Abram had developed the beginnings of a relationship. Sadie smiled to herself as she thought about how their relationship had changed in just a few days. One day Abram had been lecturing her and threatening to tell Bishop King about her secret journal, and just a few short days later, Abram and Sadie had been practically holding hands in his buggy.

Hannah Zook was getting an early start on the day's laundry, and she walked through the kitchen with a laundry basket on her hip, headed to the clothesline outside.

"Mama, I might not be home for dinner tonight," Sadie cheerfully informed her mother.

"I trust that you'll behave yourself, Sadie, yes?" Hanna gently inquired. Though she knew that Sadie, at nineteen years old, needed some freedom, Hannah still felt compelled to guide her.

"Of course, Mama," Sadie answered. "And I'll help you fold and put laundry away when I get home from work. I think I'll have enough time."

"Thank you, sweet girl," Hanna replied, as she dropped the bag of clothespins into her basket. "I'll see you this evening."

Slipping her arm through her lunch basket, Sadie followed her mother out the kitchen door and crossed the yard to the buggy she and her father would take to work. As Samuel hitched the horse to the buggy, Sadie nestled the basket beneath the seat for their ride.

"I expect I'll have the paperwork back from John Byler today, Da. I'll write out the tax checks for you to sign if Abram brings me the work." Sadie knew that her father didn't enjoy handling the paperwork side of his successful business, and Sadie was quite competent at keeping the little woodworking shop running smoothly.

A keen observer of his children and their interactions, Samuel smiled as he answered his daughter. "I'll ask Abram about the paperwork for you," Samuel said, knowing what Sadie's response would be.

"Oh I don't mind doing it," Sadie hastily responded. "I know you have to finish the chairs for the order that ships on Monday. I'll ask Abram."

Keeping quiet about the blossoming relationship between Sadie and Abram, Samuel climbed into the wagon, took the reins, and let the horse start the half-hour journey to the shop. When they arrived at Ephrata Woodworks, Abram met them in the yard to help Samuel with the horse.

"Good morning, Samuel," Abram said with a smile. "Good morning Sadie."

"Good morning, Abram," Sadie replied.

"I meant to bring you the May paperwork that Father finished, but I forgot it. It will have to wait until Monday, if that's okay."

"Oh that's fine," Sadie answered. "I have plenty to keep me busy today, anyway."

Samuel climbed down from the buggy and headed into the workshop, intending to give the two young people a little privacy. As he walked to the shop, he remembered the days he spent courting Hannah. He smiled as he thought about what it felt like to look forward to seeing Hannah each day and wondering when they could find a moment alone together.

"Can I help you with the basket," Abram asked.

"Of course. And thank you," Sadie with a smile tilted up toward the tall young man.

Abram followed Sadie to the door of the store that

displayed the beautiful and sturdy furniture that Abram and Samuel made in the workshop out back. As Sadie unlocked the door, Abram leaned ever so slightly closer to her so that he could inhale her distinctive, warm and spicy scent. Sadie noticed his movement toward her, and she turned and smiled at him.

"All set," she said quietly.

The two stepped into the showroom, and Sadie flicked on the light, powered by the generator outside. Abram carefully placed the basket on the counter, and turned to look at Sadie.

"I brought your journal back," he said, as he slipped the book from its hiding place at the waist of his pants. "I wrote a few lines, too," he finished, shyly.

"Oh, good!" Sadie exclaimed, eagerly reaching for her journal. "I'll find time to read it today."

"And I would love to go for a picnic with you this evening. It is kind of Nathan to offer to drive."

"Wonderful," Sadie replied. "I know just what I'll pack for dinner."

"I look forward to this evening, then," Abram said as he walked to the door. "Samuel will be expecting me to get back to work."

Sadie busied herself in the office, fielding a few phone calls and making sure that the furniture due to be picked up on Monday would all be ready. The day flew by, and after lunch, Nathan Kobel stopped in to see if Sadie and Abram wanted to go to the lake. Sadie thanked him for the offer and told him they were looking forward to the evening. He headed out with a promise to pick her up at six.

Sadie realized that she hadn't even had time to read Abram's entry in her journal, so when she finished dusting all of the showroom furniture, she retrieved the journal from its hiding place and settled down in one of the rocking chairs to read. As she opened the book, she realized that it had become not just her journal, but one she shared with Abram. Smiling at the thought, she found his latest writing. In typical Abram fashion, it was only a few lines.

> Sadie, when I think about you talking to such wicked men whose lives are such an abomination, I worry for your soul. You did make me think, though, that perhaps you are right that since these men are not part of our culture, that the best we can do is be polite and treat them with respect. Like you, I would not tolerate such behavior in my family or congregation, and I would shun a member who behaved so sinfully.

> Sadie, you have opened my eyes, and I can't even find the words to explain exactly how.

> I am looking forward to this evening, because I get to spend it with you.

Tears sprang to Sadie's eyes as she read Abram's thoughtful words. She was startled by his honesty and openness, and she realized that beneath the gruff exterior she'd known for her whole life that there was a sweet and tender heart. She wondered for a moment if Abram might not be the most interesting man she had ever spent time with, and she found herself wondering – briefly – if Abram might not make a good husband. Pushing the thoughts of marriage aside, Sadie retrieved her pen from behind her ear and began to write her response for Abram to read later.

❀ ❀ ❀

When Abram arrived at the Zook's house a few minutes before six o'clock that evening, he was in fine spirits. He whistled as he unhitched his horse from his sleek courting buggy, and he settled the horse in with some water and feed. As he waved to Samuel and his sons in the barn, working on their evening chores, he noticed that Sadie and Miriam were taking clothes down from the line and folding them into baskets to carry inside.

Abram, concealed from Sadie's view in the shadowed edge of the barn, indulged himself in the luxury of watching the young women while they worked. Miriam was slightly shorter than Sadie, and her light brown curls threatened to escape at any moment from the bun partially concealed by the sheer white prayer cap she wore. Both girls shared fair complexions, and Miriam's face was liberally covered with freckles from the June sunshine.

Turning his attention to the object of his affections, Abram admired Sadie's honey golden hair, a little better behaved than Miriam's, and wound in a thick braided bun beneath her prayer cap. Abram realized that his heart raced a bit when he let himself think – for just a moment – about what that mass of honey colored hair would look like when it was freed from its constraints. Realizing that his thoughts were straying into inappropriately intimate territory, Abram shook his head, stood up straight, and headed our directly across the yard to the two young women.

"Good evening Sadie, Miriam," Abram nodded at the sisters. "It looks like a perfect evening for a picnic."

Both Miriam and Sadie smiled at the obviously smitten young man. Miriam nodded to Abram and winked at Sadie.

"Good evening to you both. Sadie, if you want to leave the basket, I'll come back out for it. Be safe," Miriam prompted in her very best schoolteacher tone.

"Oh Miriam," Sadie laughed. "It's not like Abram or I will be driving. I'm sure Nathan will be very careful."

"Would you like me to help you carry the basket inside?" Abram asked Miriam.

"No, it's no trouble," the girl answered. "But thank you, Abram."

Sadie turned to Abram as Miriam headed inside with the laundry. "I would guess that Nathan will be here any minute. I'll run inside and get the picnic basket."

When Sadie returned with the basket, she and Abram sat at one of the picnic tables in the yard and waited for Nathan. Both were curious about Meredith, and they wondered what it would be like to spend the evening with a girl who wasn't even a Mennonite. They could hear Nathan's car from a good distance off, and as Sadie had already told her parents that she'd be leaving shortly, she and Abram got in the backseat of the car, and Nathan drove away.

Steering the car from the drive to the road, Nathan handled the introductions.

"It's very nice to meet you both," Meredith politely declared, as she gave a little wave from the front seat. "I've been asking Nathan lots of questions about the Amish, and he's told me that you won't mind if I ask you a few too. If that ok?"

Abram thought for a second and started to answer, but Meredith chattered on without even waiting for his response.

"I've only lived in Ephrata for a year, and I've seen lots of Amish buggies, and I love shoofly pie, but I've never really gotten to talk to an Amish. So what's it like?"

Nathan chuckled and reached over to put his hand on Meredith's tanned knee. "Meredith, give them a chance to breathe. And I told you that they're Plain. They don't use the word 'Amish.'"

Meredith giggled and turned to face the couple in the back seat. "I'm so sorry. You're gonna think I'm rude, and I'm really not. I'm just curious. That's why my dad always tells me that I'm a born reporter. I wrote for the school newspaper last year, and I'd love to write for the New York Times or another big city paper."

Meredith continued her cheerful and nonstop chatter, while Abram and Sadie just looked at one another, a little stunned by the sheer volume of words that spilled from the girl's lips. They'd never heard so many words so fast in their lives. Sadie gave Abram a little shrug and smile, and they were content to listen to the vivacious Meredith.

Abram's glance fell on Nathan's hand, still lightly touching Meredith's bare knee. He was transfixed by the intimate physical contact and by the girl's exposed skin. No stranger to the facts of life, having grown up around farm animals, Abram had nevertheless been quite sheltered from bare skin for his entire life. That a girl could be at once so exposed and so comfortable was just astounding. He also couldn't help but imagine what that smooth skin must feel like under Nathan's fingertips. How could Nathan possibly concentrate on driving the car when he had that irresistibly distracting sensation? Abram couldn't honestly tell if he felt envy for Nathan's ease with Meredith or pity for Nathan's focus on sensual pleasures. Having been told his entire life that attraction wasn't a solid basis for a relationship, Abram was utterly unable to understand how you could keep your focus on anything other than attraction with so much bare skin so close.

Realizing that he was staring, Abram waited for a break in Meredith's stream of words. When she finally paused, Abram spoke up from the back seat. "Nathan, I thank you for your offer to drive. It is a treat for us to get to go to the lake. It would have taken until tomorrow morning in my buggy."

Nathan made eye contact with Abram in the rearview mirror. "You're welcome, man. I know what it's like to want to get out from under your parents' roof every once in a while."

Sadie smiled at the easy conversation between the two young men, for she had witnessed less-than-cordial exchanges before. She started to describe the dinner she had packed in the picnic basket, and before they knew it, the car had arrived at Speedwell Forge Lake.

Chapter Twelve

Abram, Sadie, Nathan, and Meredith were lazily sprawled on the enormous blanket that Nathan had pulled from his trunk. They'd devoured nearly every bite of the dinner Sadie had packed, and Meredith rolled over to the cooler she'd packed with iced tea, bottles of water, and soft drinks.

"I have a surprise for dessert," she announced, pulling a bottle of wine from the cooler.

Abram instantly tensed up, and started to protest.

Nathan took the lead, though, and explained to Meredith that Plain folk typically don't drink.

"I know. That's why I picked out this wine. It's a Moscato d'Asti. It's from Italy, and it's sweet, and light, and it doesn't have much alcohol in it. It won't hurt to have a little sip."

"I'll have some," Nathan declared, reaching for a plastic cup.

"Thank you, but I will pass," Abram said, waving off the cup that Nathan offered."

"Sadie?" Meredith asked.

"I believe that I will have a little taste," Sadie answered deliberately. "Not too much, please."

Sadie took a sip of the chilled, sweet wine and looked up with a startled expression. "It has bubbles," she exclaimed with delight.

Meredith laughed. "Yes. It's frizzante, which means it has bubbles, but isn't as bubbly as Champagne."

Nathan looked at Meredith. "I don't know that Abram and Sadie will have much interest in becoming wine experts." Turning to the Plain couple, Nathan explained. "Meredith's father is a wine importer. He goes to France and Italy a few times every year to taste and purchase wine."

"Wow," remarked Sadie. "I don't know about any other wines, but this one is delicious. It tastes like Spring."

Nathan stood up and stretched. "Anyone feel like a walk?"

"I'll go," Meredith answered, looking to Abram and Sadie for their decisions.

"I'd like to stay and just relax," decided Abram.

"I'll stay too," answered Sadie. "I'm enjoying watching the swallows swooping down and catching bugs over the lake."

Reaching out to take Meredith's hand, Nathan pretended to be stern. "You kids behave, now," he said, as he and Meredith began their stroll around the lake.

"Would you like a taste?" Sadie asked Abram, as she offered her cup to him. "It's delicious, and it's not like one sip will hurt you."

Abram reached out, took the cup and took a tiny taste. "You're right," he said with surprise. "It's delicious." Abram thought for a moment. "My mother always told me that drinking alcohol was a sin and that it tasted bad. She may have been right about the sin part, but this tasted wonderful."

"I am sure that she was just concerned for your soul," Sadie said.

"I am sure you are right," Abram agreed. "But why would she tell me something that is not true? If being drunk is wrong, regardless of what the wine tastes like, then it would be better to be truthful, I think."

"That is an interesting thing to say," Sadie said thoughtfully.

"It is just that I have had reason to think of late. Reading your journal has made me think about everything a little differently."

Sadie blushed prettily. "Really, Abram? When I started writing, I never even thought that anyone else would read what I wrote. It has only been over the last couple of weeks that I've had an audience."

"It's just that you see things differently than I do."

Sadie looked alarmed, and Abram continued in a rush.

"It's just that I didn't know that it was possible to be Plain and still think about the English as you do. You somehow show them what it is like to live Plain, while still treating them with respect."

"I sometimes wonder if I am being too worldly when I think about the Englishers I meet," Sadie confided to

Abram. "But sometimes I think I learn lessons from them, and I think that maybe it makes me more humble."

"I thought that what you wrote about the men in the shop was interesting. I'm not sure how I would have behaved, but your example makes me ashamed to think of how I might have treated those men. Sadie, you have made me think. And while I would guess that my mother and father would tell me it is wrong, I enjoy thinking about the things you write about."

Abram took the last little sip of the wine Sadie had handed him, and he shifted his position to recline and face Sadie.

Sadie smiled at Abram and enjoyed being able to look at him without having to worry about people around her noticing. She studied him – his straw hat shading his warm, brown eyes from the evening sun. Although he watched her Sadie boldly decided to continue her examination of his form. She looked at his strong, clean-shaven jawline, and wondered what he would look like with the beginnings of a married man's beard.

She let her gaze drop to his broad shoulders, and though she knew that marriages weren't based on physical attraction, she indulged herself and contemplated what his shoulders would look like if he removed his shirt. The skin would be pale, of course, since it never saw the sun. She wondered if his skin would be smooth or covered with hair. She traced the line of his suspenders to the waist of his black pants and decided she'd gone more than far enough.

Abram watched Sadie's eyes return to his, and he

was surprised at the frank and admiring expression on her face. He knew – at least he was learning – about her sweet, pure heart, but the look in her eyes was one of desire. Knowing that desire could lead to selfish, destructive behavior, and being wholly unfamiliar with what it felt like to have a woman look at him the way that Sadie was, Abram pushed himself up from his elbow, and sat up straight.

"Would you like to go for a walk?"

"No," Sadie answered. "I think I would like to write for a few minutes if you don't mind. I have some thoughts I would like to share with you, but I would rather write them down for you to read later."

"That is fine. I'm happy just to stay here and listen to the birds," Abram replied. He stretched out and laid down on the blanket, his hat tipped forward to shade his face from the sun, and his hands crossed behind his head. Abram sighed as he settled in. He didn't have very many moments in his life when he had the luxury of being idle and quiet. He watched Sadie as she reached into the picnic basket to retrieve her journal, pulled the pen from behind her ear, and sat cross-legged to write. Realizing that staring at Sadie wasn't going to be a relaxing pastime, Abram closed his eyes and enjoyed the feeling of the last sunshine of the day.

Sadie wrote a few more lines in her journal, thinking about Abram reading it later. She wasn't quite sure what to do about the feelings she was having, but she knew she'd better distract herself. After she'd written for a few minutes, she looked up to see Meredith and

Nathan walking hand in hand along the far side of the lake. As Sadie watched, Meredith stopped, faced Nathan, and kissed him. Sadie's eyes widened as she watched the couple. She was so unused to seeing public displays of affection that she didn't know what to think. This kiss was clearly a different sort from the kiss the Plain people used to greet one another at church services.

Flustered and a little embarrassed, Sadie turned to Abram to suggest that they clean up and repack the picnic basket, and she found him looking right at her. He had clearly seen the kiss, as he was looking at her mouth, his lips slightly parted. Sadie smiled, knowing that Abram couldn't help but see the curve of her mouth. At least she didn't need to wonder if he was feeling the same attraction she was struggling with. Though Abram had just eaten dinner, he looked like he wanted to devour her lips.

"Abram?" Sadie said quietly.

Flinching as if he'd been pinched, Abram regarded Sadie with a guilty expression.

"Yes?"

"Do you mind helping me collect our things and repack the basket?"

"Of course," Abram answered, as he stood up and stretched his tall frame after his brief rest.

"If I give you my journal tonight, will you be able to bring it back to me on Sunday?" Sadie asked.

The congregation that the Byler and Zook families belonged to met every other week in the home of one of its members. The day after tomorrow was to be the

Zook's day to host, and although Sadie knew the house would be full to bursting with the twenty or so families in their membership, she hoped that Abram could manage to discreetly slip the book to her. It had become one of the things she most looked forward to – this exchange of the journal and the shared writing.

"I believe I can do that," Abram answered, as he handed the stack of plates to Sadie so that she could pack them in the basket. By the time Meredith and Nathan returned to the blanket, the picnic basket had been neatly repacked, and Abram and Sadie were sharing a bottle of water.

"Nathan has told me that I can ask you a few questions about being Amish…I mean Plain… as long as I don't drive you crazy," Meredith exclaimed, as she sat on the blanket and crossed her tan legs in front of her."

Abram and Sadie looked at one another, and Abram, thinking of Sadie's attitude toward the English, answered. "Okay."

Excited to begin, Meredith jumped right in. "So you both work at your father's shop, Sadie. Do you both get paid?"

Sadie answered the first in what she expected would be a barrage of questions to follow. "Yes. Abram and I both get paid. I am saving some money for when I get married so that I can buy some things I will need to set up a house. I won't have to be a burden on my husband."

"And I, too, am saving money to be able to build a house when I marry," Abram added.

"Do you wish you had gone to school longer than just eighth grade?"

"I had learned everything I needed to know by that point," Abram answered. "Now I learn every day how to run a business to provide for my family. I have no need of more than that."

"Sadie?" Meredith asked. "Did you want more of an education?"

"For a while I thought maybe I did. I love to read, and I thought it would be wonderful to go to college, like Nathan will in a few months, and have so much information everywhere I looked." Sadie paused, thoughtful. "I realized, though, that my desire for more education was a vanity. A selfish desire that would only serve to distance me from the way I love and the people I love. It would have made it too hard to be Plain, and that is who I am."

Meredith looked at Sadie, remarkably quiet for a few moments. "I have never thought of it that way," she said.

"You done?" Nathan asked Meredith with a smile.

"Oh you know me!" she answered with a giggle. "I'm never finished asking questions. Do you ever wish you had electricity?"

Sadie laughed as she answered. "We have generators at home and at the shop. We have a refrigerator, and we even have electric lights in most of our rooms. We don't use public power, but we can make our own."

"We don't have electricity," Abram said. "We use gas for our stove and ovens, but we use lanterns and candles for light."

"So you don't all live exactly the same?" Meredith asked, surprised. "Why do your families do things differently?"

"My parents have always believed that the simplest life is the best. They believe that too many conveniences will make us proud and too worldly. I have always believed that they were right, the stricter, the better. Now, I am not so sure."

Sadie was shocked at Abram's answer. The Byler family was one of a handful that practiced the very strictest interpretation of the *Ordnung*, but it had never occurred to her that Abram might question his parents' choices.

"Do you argue with your parents?" Meredith asked Abram.

"No." Abram stood up and extended his hand to Sadie to help her get up from the blanket. "I have enjoyed this evening, but it is time that we head back home. I may need to help my father with chores."

"Abram, I didn't mean to be rude. I'm terrible about going on and on and asking questions about things that are none of my business."

"You were not rude, Meredith. Arguing with our parents just isn't our way," Abram answered, clearly wanting to end the conversation.

Nathan grabbed the edge of the blanket after everyone had moved from it, and he gestured with a nod that Sadie should take the opposite edge. They folded the blanket, stowed it in the trunk of the car, packed up the cooler and basket, and were ready to leave in just a few minutes.

"Nathan, I can't thank you enough for this evening," Sadie sighed when everything had been put away. "It was such a treat to have a relaxing night with no dishes to do and no chores to finish. We're hosting church on Sunday, so tomorrow will be extra busy all day."

"You're welcome, Sadie," Nathan answered. "It was nice to get to know Abram a little better. He always seemed like such a serious dude, like it would kill him to smile, but he's actually pretty cool."

"Hmm," Sadie echoed. "Pretty cool, huh?" The words felt strange in her mouth, like she was speaking as someone else.

The ride back to Sadie's house was fairly quiet, but not awkward. Each of the young people seemed to be thinking through the evening they'd just spent, and they were content to just ride in silence. When Nathan pulled into Sadie's yard and stopped the car, Meredith turned in her seat to face Abram and Sadie.

"It was so nice to meet you both, and I hope you'll forgive my being so nosy."

"It was nice to meet you too," replied Abram. "And you have nothing to apologize for."

Sadie and Abram got out, retrieved the picnic basket from the trunk, and waved at Meredith and Nathan as they drove off into the dark June evening. While Abram held the basket, Sadie stepped toward him. Uncertain about her intention, Abram stepped back, as if he were afraid of her getting too close to him.

"I'm not going to bite, Abram," Sadie said with a smile. "I just want to get my journal out of the basket."

"Oh." Abram looked sheepish and held the basket while Sadie fished out the little cloth-covered book.

"I can't remember when I've had such a lovely evening, Abram," she said softly, as she handed the book to the young man. "I'll be busy getting ready for church on Sunday, but I look forward to seeing you."

"I look forward to it as well. Perhaps we can go for a walk after church, if you don't have other plans?"

"I would love to."

The pair bid each other good night, and Abram hitched his horse to his buggy as Sadie walked to the house. Turning in the kitchen doorway, she waved at the young man as he climbed into the buggy.

Chapter Thirteen

Abram rinsed his paintbrush and stretched his sore muscles. Rising before dawn as usual, he'd spent a long, hard day working around his family's home. After his usual chores, he and Joshua had taken advantage of the warm, dry weather forecast for the next few days and had repainted the fencing around their property. Working steadily with his brother, each on one side of the fencing, they had just finished painting the last section of fence in time to wash up for dinner. Abram looked forward to going to bed early, reading Sadie's journal, safely stashed beneath his pillow, and writing a response to her. He wasn't quite sure how he'd manage to get the journal to her on Sunday, but he planned to find a way.

Startled from his reverie by cold water washing over his face, Abram scowled at his younger brother and used his paintbrush to sling water back at the young man who clearly expected retaliation. The icy cold well water felt so good after the hot and sweaty work, so the brothers continued splashing and yelling at one another until both were soaked to the skin. Wet clothes sticking to skin, both boys knew they would have to change into dry clothes before their mother would allow them at the dinner table.

"Mother hasn't rung the dinner bell yet," Joshua said, shaking his head to scatter water drops. "If we hurry, we can go in through the front door and get changed before she can get mad at us for tracking water into the kitchen."

"Good thinking, Joshua. It is worth a try."

Quickly sealing and storing their paint cans and brushes, the boys walked around to the little used front door that opened into the entryway, between the parlor and the dining room. They hoped to evade Ruth's eagle eye and sharp tongue. Joshua slowly opened the door – fortunately noiseless on its well-oiled hinges, and stuck his head inside to assess the situation.

"I don't see anyone," Joshua whispered to his brother. "Let's go."

Joshua stepped inside first, just as Sarah entered the dining room with a stack of plates from the kitchen. She opened her mouth to speak, but Joshua frantically shook his head, with his finger at his lips. Quickly assessing the situation – two dripping brothers in the entryway – she grinned, shook her head, and waved them upstairs. Just as the Abram put his foot on the first stair step, Sarah caught his attention and gestured to he puddles of water on the floor. Silently assuring her that he'd clean up the water, Abram followed his brother up the steps.

Grinning at his brother at their having evaded Ruth, Abram opened the door to his bedroom to get a set of dry clothing. He stopped dead in his tracks when he saw his bed had been stripped of sheets and blankets. He knew without a doubt that there was no way on earth that Sadie's journal would have escaped the notice of whichever of the girls had taken the sheets off his bed to be laundered.

As he rushed toward the bed, hoping that the journal was still in its place beneath his pillow, he hoped desperately that it had been Sarah, rather than Ruth, or even Katie, who had found the book. He moved his pillow and there was no journal. Casting his glance around the room, he knew that his hopes of finding the book somewhere in the room were completely unfounded. The simple, Spartan room held no hiding places. The book was gone.

Forgetting for a moment that his clothes were soaking wet, Abram sat heavily on the edge of his bed. Absolutely panicked, he figured that his best hope was that somehow it had been Sarah who'd been assigned to strip the beds, and that somehow, some way, she would have decided to keep his secret. It wasn't a completely crazy thought. He couldn't even begin to fathom how awful it would be if his mother had found the journal. Realizing that he had gotten the bed wet, he stood up and decided that he would hope for the best, try to get Sarah aside privately, and push the thoughts of his mother with Sadie's journal out of his head.

Hearing the dinner bell ring from downstairs, Abram hurriedly changed into dry clothes, combed through his hair with his fingers, and headed downstairs, apprehensive and uncertain. Meeting Joshua in the hall, he envied his brother's easy grin at having escaped their mother's wrath. Remembering to bring a towel with him to wipe up the wet floor, Abram thought that the only good thing was that if Ruth had the journal, he would know immediately. He couldn't imagine his mother staying quiet, especially as he thought about Sadie's last entry in the journal. Of all the things for his mother to read, none could be worse than that one. There was no way she'd understand.

Successfully drying the floor, Abram joined the rest of the family in the kitchen. Hopefully examining Sarah's face for hints and finding none, Abram looked around the room. Katie was occupied with stirring a pitcher of tea; Joshua and little John were bringing in two dining chairs that John had repaired earlier that day, John washed his hands at the sink, and that left only Ruth.

Terrified at what he would see in her face, Abram turned to look at his mother, and he knew instantly. Her gaze held thunder. She watched him steadily, as if she were looking to corroborate what she surely felt was damning information contained in Sadie's little book. Ruth didn't say a word, but Abram knew that the peaceful Saturday evening that he had looked forward to was not in his future.

John finished washing his hands, and left the kitchen for the dining room, silently indicating that dinner would begin shortly. As the boys filed into the dining room, Abrams heart was in his shoes. He knew without a doubt that his evening would be unpleasant.

The silent prayer over, the meal began without a word. Dishes were passed, plates filled and emptied, and the only sounds at the table were those from silverware touching plates. Each time Abram looked around the table, he found his family members self-consciously staring at their plates, looking up only infrequently. The discomfort hung over the table and was almost tangible. Ruth, from her seat nearest the kitchen was the sole family member who seemed unruffled, her gaze never wavering from Abram. She didn't touch a bite of her dinner. She simply glared at her son.

Katie, typically a bubbly chatterbox, leaned over to Sarah and quietly asked, "What is wrong with Mother? Is she angry with Abram? What has he done?"

Sarah quieted her sister with a quick shake of her head, and the silence descended again. After what seemed like the longest and most awkward meal of his life, John stood to indicate the meal's end.

"Abram," he said without making eye contact with his son. "Your mother and I will talk to you after dinner is cleaned up."

Abram's chin dropped to his chest. Not only had his mother found the book, but also she had spoken to his father. Abram knew with certainty that there were only two possible paths for the conversation ahead. He could either take his parents' criticism and beg for their forgiveness, or he could stand up for himself. As he sat at the table, momentarily unable to move, he thought about what to do.

If he had done wrong, if he had sinned, then the right thing to do would be to accept responsibility for his behavior and suffer the consequences. If it had been wrong to keep Sadie's secret, and even worse, to participate in the private writing they had shared, then he should meekly accept the judgment of John and Ruth.

But Abram didn't think he had sinned. He had thought and prayed for weeks, and he was convinced that not only was Sadie not wrong for keeping a journal, but she was actually using the talents that God had given her in a wholesome, good way. Abram knew in his heart that he and Sadie had been pure in their behavior. Though Abram also knew that his thoughts hadn't been entirely pure with regard to the growing desire that he felt for Sadie, he also knew that he would never act on that passion before it was right to do so.

Pushing his chair back from the table, Abram's biggest regret was that his mother had found the journal on this particular day. Had she read the journal on any other day, she still would have been displeased, but when he remembered the content of the last few lines Sadie had written as they sat on the picnic blanket, looking at the lake, Abram knew that there was no way he would be able to convince his parents of the innocence and purity of his relationship with Sadie. Deciding that he had no choice but to listen and try to remain calm, Abram left the dining room and walked slowly into the parlor, the room his parents had always used when they found it necessary to discipline one of their children.

Abram sat on a chair that he had made at Samuel Zook's shop, leaving a loveseat and several other chairs open. The parlor was dark, as no one had lit the oil lamps. Abram figured that his mother and father would light them if necessary. Abram wasn't quite sure if he should try to prepare himself for the conversation, or if he should just let his parents take the lead. He supposed he would have to just figure it out.

A few minutes passed, and Abram could hear the sounds of dishes being put away in cupboards. He watched in silence as his mother and father entered the parlor. His father lit two lamps, and his parents seated themselves on the loveseat facing Abram. Abram's eyes were fixed on the journal in his mother's hands, and he forced himself to meet her eyes with a cool, steady gaze.

Ruth opened the book and began to read.

"Abram, I will never forget this evening. The warm summer evening, watching you take your first sip of wine, and answering all the questions about being Plain. I am so glad that my writing has made you think, as your writing has helped me get to know you in a way that I never had before."

John Byler shifted his gaze from his wife to his son. "Abram, we have always trusted you, and we have always believed that you had been raised to be properly Plain. Your mother and I have read everything in this book, and it is clear that you have lost your faith. It is not right to be thinking about the wickedness of the world. We live apart because you can't be Plain and live in the world."

Ruth picked up the sermon. "Abram, this wicked girl has polluted your heart and mind. She puts evil thoughts about gay men in your head. You go out with people who make you question your faith. And of all people, that

Nathan Kobel! He will turn out just as rotten as his father did before him, mark my words. You drink wine, and you are a sinner because of Sadie Zook. You will not write to her again. You will not drive her home from church. You will not go around with her. You will set your sights on a modest girl with a Plain heart and a pure mind. Sadie Zook is not that girl."

Abram's eyes widened as his mother's tirade continued. When she paused to take a breath, he opened his mouth to speak.

John held up a hand to stop Abram. "We are not finished. There is not a word you can say that alters what has happened. Abram, your community and your family depend on your following of the *ordnung*. You have been baptized. You are a member of the church. Ruth and I have discussed it, and unless there is more that we do not know, we believe that you do not need to make a confession to the Elder, but you must end this sinful relationship with Sadie."

Ruth closed the book on her lap. "Abram, you have made your commitment to the church. You have made the decision as an adult to follow the *ordnung*. Sadie has not. A girl like Sadie – one who spends all her energy thinking about worldly Englishers who commit such disgusting sins, a girl who drinks wine with you, she is not the kind of girl you can marry and remain with us. She will be shunned, mark my words. She will be tempted beyond what her weak will can bear. She will leave you to live in the world or she will convince you to leave with her. You will end up alone, or you will end up shunned along with Sadie."

Abram was stunned by his parents' words. He knew in his heart that they misunderstood Sadie, and they misunderstood their relationship. He tried again to speak, and again was stopped by his father.

John stood, clearly intending to put an end to the discussion. "Your mother and I agree. You will no longer see Sadie Zook outside of work, and you will stay home from church tomorrow. We plan to speak with Samuel and Hannah after church. They must know what Sadie has wrapped herself up in. Samuel would not want his daughter talking to gay men, and Sadie should have known that. We will not have you corrupted or ripped away from the church and your family because of Sadie. We will hear you confess your sins, if you want, but we will not discuss this further."

Finally unable to restrain himself any longer, Abram jumped to his feet. Never before had he defied his parents, but he was so certain that he had committed no sins that he could no longer keep quiet. "You are wrong. You don't understand Sadie at all."

"Abram Byler," warned his mother. "You will not speak to us in that way. Do you deny what is in this book?" Ruth brandished the journal, shaking it in Abram's direction.

Abram took a deep breath and tried to calm himself. Displays of temper were a sign of pride and a lack of control. He sat down on the chair. "Mother, every word in that journal is true. You do not understand it though.

If you would let me explain it to you. If you would let me explain Sadie to you..."

Ruth shook her head. "Abram, you do not understand the danger of falling in love with an outsider."

"But Sadie isn't an outsider. I have known her my entire life. Father, you have done the bookkeeping for Samuel for longer than I have been alive!"

John took a step toward his son. "Abram, you will have to trust us. Your mother and I know of the heartache, the loss that comes with being shunned by your family and you community."

"But Father, you do not understand." Abram realized that he was repeating himself, but he couldn't think of any other way to approach the discussion without getting angry and losing his temper. "I don't want to leave the community and neither does Sadie. If you would let me explain, then you would see that she..."

Ruth stood up, the journal clutched so tightly that her fingers were white against the journal's yellow fabric. "You have to know that this is for the best. People like the Kobels and like Sadie will stain your reputation and will lead you astray. I will not see you ruin your life over this girl. You will obey us, Abram. You will."

Unwilling to listen to another word, Ruth left the parlor. John looked at his son, as if he could somehow read Abram's mind and intentions if he studied long enough. Without another word, John followed his wife out of the room, and Abram was left alone. Realizing that everything he'd been taught his whole life compelled him to obey his parents, he slumped back in the chair and covered his face with his hands.

Furious and frustrated, Abram sat in the parlor and tried to figure out what God would have him do. Could he have been wrong about Sadie? Were his parents right that she should concern herself less with the world and more with being humble? He also wondered what his parents would say to Samuel and Hannah. When Abram remembered that his mother still had Sadie's journal, he was just beside himself. Whatever Ruth had planned to do with the book could not end well for Sadie. Thinking for a second that he could possibly talk his parents into returning the journal to him, Abram quickly realized that there was no chance of their giving the little volume up.

Abram knew for certain that a storm was brewing and headed straight for Sadie Zook, and he was completely powerless to stop it.

Chapter Fourteen

Sunday dawned gray and drizzling rain. The Zook clan had been up since well before sunrise preparing for the hundred and fifteen churchgoers who were expected in just a few hours. Sadie and Miriam had washed every window in the house the day before, and they'd laundered all the curtains as well, while Esther had dusted the house from top to bottom and helped in the kitchen. Hannah had been busily baking for a couple of days. Though the Sunday meal wasn't elaborate – sliced meats and cheeses for sandwiches, there were an awful lot of mouths to feed.

Samuel and his boys had brought the church wagon with the benches for seating everyone, and they'd neatened up the barn and the yard so there would be plenty of room for all of the horses and buggies that would crowd the place. Sunday morning saw them tending their animals, collecting eggs from the chickens, and picking the strawberries that seemed to ripen overnight in the warm June weather.

Sadie worked happily in the kitchen with her mother and sisters as they prepared breakfast. Sadie was hungry and knew that she'd be glad of a big breakfast as she would be sitting through the long church service as well as beginning her instruction that would lead to her baptism in a few months. She wasn't the least bit apprehensive about making the commitment to become a full member of the church, as she felt safe, secure, and fulfilled by her church family.

Some of Sadie's good mood was because she knew that in just a few hours she would see Abram. Peering out the window and hoping that the weather would clear so that they could go for a walk after church, Sadie finished cutting out biscuits and put them in the oven.

"All done, Mama," she said cheerfully. "Shall I go ring the bell for the boys?"

Hannah looked at the clock and figured that by the time the biscuits were done, the boys would have had time to wash up and be seated. "Yes, Sadie."

Breakfast was a little more hurried than usual, as all of the Zooks needed to get cleaned up from their morning chores and put on their best clothing for church before the congregation arrived. While the ladies washed dishes and neatened the dining room and kitchen, the boys set up the benches that filled the living room and even spilled into the dining room.

Finally clean, dressed, and ready, Samuel noticed the first buggy arriving and sent young Samuel out to coordinate the parking and care of horses. All of the men headed outside to greet the arrivals, while the women stayed in the kitchen to handle all the food that would be arriving for the communal meal after worship. Sadie perked up when she noticed little Katie Byer running by the kitchen window, tearing around the yard with other children. Parents usually encouraged the activity since there were several hours ahead for children to sit quietly.

Eagerly watching for Abram, Sadie reached for the tray of sliced ham and beef that Sarah Byler held and greeted her with a smile. "I expect Abram will have driven separately?"

Sarah didn't quite know what to say to Sadie. She didn't know exactly what John and Ruth had discussed with Abram the evening before, but she had heard Sadie's name from the other room. Ruth's tone had not been complimentary. "Um," Sarah hesitated. "Um. I'm not sure if he's coming." Sarah pushed the tray toward Sadie and practically ran from the kitchen into the living room that was quickly filling with the women arriving.

Perplexed, Sadie put the tray into the refrigerator and wondered why Abram wasn't there. Could he be sick? Hoping she would have a chance to ask Sarah what the problem was, Sadie handled tray after tray of food before she could escape the kitchen. Straightening her bonnet and smoothing her dress, Sadie entered the dining room to survey the people inside: mostly women, as the men typically greeted one another outside. Sadie scanned the room for Sarah. She saw Ruth and Sarah both, seated side by side, Ruth's rigid frame and narrow shoulders facing the front of the room as if she expected the service to begin any second.

Sadie sighed, frustrated because she had never particularly warmed to Abram's mother. She knew it wasn't right to dislike a member of her congregation, but Ruth always seemed so sour and unpleasant, particularly toward the younger girls of the membership. Sadie had hoped to corner Sarah privately, but that obviously wouldn't happen. It was odd, too, as Sadie looked around the room, that Ruth and Sarah had been seated so early, as the adult women were still greeting one another. Each of the baptized members exchanged solemn, chaste kisses with one another – women indoors, and men outdoors, but Ruth and Sarah appeared to have opted not to participate.

Thinking that perhaps Abram was sick, and his family didn't want to spread any of the sickness to other members, Sadie made her way over to her mother. "Mama, did you talk to Ruth Byler?" Sadie whispered to Hannah.

Hannah turned to her daughter and replied quietly. "No. Ruth didn't speak to anyone. She just sat down and hasn't moved. She looks to be angry."

Sadie wondered for a second how anyone could tell if Ruth was angry, since she always had such a sour expression, but she chided herself on her uncharitable thoughts.

Hannah put a hand on Sadie's arm. "I'll go greet her and see if anything is wrong."

Sadie stood back against the living room wall and watched as Hannah made her way across to Ruth. Hannah seated herself on the open space next to Ruth on the backless bench and leaned forward for a holy kiss.

Sadie gasped aloud as Ruth turned her cheek, refusing Hannah's greeting. Ruth turned to Sarah, spoke a few words, and Sarah rose and left the two women alone. Ruth bent in toward Hannah, her thin shoulders shaking in anger as Ruth briefly spoke.

Hannah leaned back as if she were surprised, and Sadie saw her mother's eyes seek out her own. Hannah looked shocked and displeased, and she spoke a few words to Ruth and stood up. Sadie was perplexed. Clearly what Ruth told Hannah involved Sadie, and clearly it had displeased Hannah. Sadie headed toward her mother as the men began to filter into the room.

Hannah reached Sadie's side and looked at her daughter as if she didn't recognize her. Hannah sat on one of the benches on the women's side of the room, and she grabbed Sadie's hand and pulled her down to sit next to her. Hannah leaned over. "What have you done to upset Ruth Byler, Sadie?"

"Nothing, Mama!" Sadie whispered.

"Well, she is furious at you about something and she and John want to talk to me and Samuel after church. If you've done something wrong, it is better to confess it to me now, Sadie."

"Mama, truly, I have done nothing wrong. I don't know why she is angry."

Hannah reached out and laid her hand on top of Sadie's. "Then I am sure it will be fine, Sadie. Let us clear our minds and listen to God."

Sadie tried her best to calm her thoughts and get her emotions under control. She and her mother sat near the front of the room, and Sadie could practically feel Ruth's eyes on her. Turning around to scan the room for Abram, Sadie tried unsuccessfully to avoid Ruth's piercing glare from near the dining room. Uncomfortable, Sadie turned back around to face the front as the preacher began speaking.

It was as though the sermons had been specially ordered for her, Sadie thought. The first sermon was an admonition about simplicity and how cluttering your life with too many distractions took time and energy from nobler, purer pursuits. Sadie had wondered many times if her writing served as a distraction from more important tasks, but she had prayed about her writing so many times that the answer was written on her heart. She was careful to use her writing as a means of relating her religion to her everyday life. If anything, her journal kept her focus where it should be – on the righteousness of her behavior.

After a few songs and prayers, the second sermon frightened Sadie a bit. The preacher spoke about the need for vigilance among Plain people. He urged the congregation to look not just at their own behavior, but also at the behavior of their neighbors. Keeping a community pure required the efforts of every member, and ensuring the health of the church meant rooting out evil, wherever it grew. Sadie paled when the preacher read from Matthew 5:29: "And if thy right eye offend thee, pluck it out, and cast *it* from thee: for it is profitable for thee that one of thy members should perish, and not *that* thy whole body should be cast into hell." Shivering to think of Ruth

Byler's response to the verse, Sadie found that she nearly welcomed the end of the service so that whatever Ruth's grievance was could be resolved.

The third and final sermon helped Sadie feel some confidence in the face of the impending confrontation. The preacher, Sadie's own father, urged the congregation to use their talents for the glory of God. He exhorted the membership to follow their pure inclinations and find ways to ensure that their talents were used, rather than wasted. Most important, though, was the necessity of using one's talents for good. Sadie felt strengthened when her father read from the parable of the talents, and her heart was warmed by the knowledge the God gave talents and demanded that they be invested, rather than squandered.

Sitting up a little straighter during the final hymns and prayers, Sadie felt a calm and a peace descend over her. She felt for a moment as though she were looking at herself from above, and she saw a young woman on the brink of adulthood, whose heart was pure, and whose conscience was clear. She realized that whatever John and Ruth Byler were worked up over, that she needn't concern herself. God saw into her heart, and he knew that Sadie had done no wrong. Resolving to handle herself with grace and generosity of spirit, Sadie knew that she could handle anything that Ruth Byler might throw her way.

When the service ended, Sadie and three other young people moved to sit in front of one of the preachers to begin their instruction for the baptisms that would occur in about a month. The other women rose to prepare for the meal. Since the drizzle outside had turned into a steady light rain, it wouldn't be possible to eat outside, so the men would eat first, and the women would take a second shift. Most of the benches were moved to the sides of the room, and some were used as makeshift tables to feed the crowd. Sadie looked for Ruth, planning to calmly make eye contact, but the thin woman was nowhere to be found.

The men ate, stood from the tables, and retreated to the barn, leaving the women to clear and reset places for the remaining hungry worshipers. Scanning the room, Sadie still didn't see Ruth Byler, but she did see Hannah, so she knew that the confrontation between the Bylers and the Zooks wasn't going on right that moment. Sadie chose to eat lightly, as she still felt a little anxiety about Ruth's anger.

After everyone had eaten, and after the women had cleaned up, washed dishes, and packed up the leftovers, the church members started to disperse a little earlier than usual. The rain had picked up, and most folks wanted to get home before the storm worsened. Sadie felt completely at loose ends, not sure what she should do. Finally, there was just a single buggy in the yard, and Ruth Byler, skirts soaked, descended from the buggy with a book in her hand.

Ruth crossed the yard, joined by John and Samuel coming from the barn. She entered the kitchen, water streaming from her bonnet, and she looked at Sadie without saying a word. When John and Samuel came inside, Samuel put a hand on Sadie's shoulder and spoke softly.

"Sadie, we need to have a word with you in the parlor."

Ruth looked at Samuel with shock. "That girl does not deserve to be present for this. She has already spoken for herself. You will see."

Samuel looked at John. "John, Sadie is my daughter, and if this conversation concerns her, she will be a part of it."

"As you say, Samuel."

Hannah joined Ruth, John, Samuel, and Sadie in the parlor. Sadie sat in her favorite bent wood rocking chair; her parents sat together on a loveseat, and they gestured to another loveseat, indicating that the Bylers should be seated. John sat, but Ruth was clearly too upset. She paced back and forth near the doorway, leaving little puddles of water on the floor.

Hannah noticed Ruth's distress, and stood. "Ruth, let me get you some towels. You're soaked to the skin."

"No, Hannah. This won't take long, and I want to get out of this house. Let us say our piece, and we'll be on our way.

Hannah slowly sat back down, clearly stunned by the Ruth's venom-laced words. Samuel met her eyes and decided to try to handle the discussion in a calm fashion.

"John," Samuel began. "What is all this about?"

John cleared his throat and took a deep breath. "Samuel and Hannah, I am sure you know that our Abram has been spending some time with Sadie of late. We have known you both for many years, and though we have some differences in the way we live our lives, we have always thought of you as friends." He paused and thought of how best to continue.

Ruth was unable to stop herself from interrupting. "But your daughter has been keeping secrets from you." Ruth waved Sadie's journal in front of her. "She has been writing in secret – hiding her foolish and selfish and proud behavior because she knows it is wrong! She writes about sin and the English and she has tempted our son." Ruth's pace picked up, and her volume increased as she was increasingly carried away by emotion. "She has brought him together with that terrible Kobel boy, and she has been riding around in cars and drinking wine!"

"Ruth Byler!" Samuel interrupted. "Please sit down and calm yourself. We will listen to all you have to say, but please calm your temper."

"Come sit, Ruth. There is a proper way to address these problems, and we need to be mindful of our behavior." John patted the loveseat, and gestured to his wife to join him.

Ruth crossed the room and sat, bowing her head and making an effort to calm down. "Samuel, Hannah, this book is Sadie's journal. I don't know how Abram came to have it, but Sadie has been writing about her dealings with the English for months, maybe longer."

Samuel turned to Sadie. He looked at his daughter who sat upright in the rocking chair, her hands folded together, only the whitened knuckles betraying her tension. "Is this true, Sadie? Is this book full of your writing?"

"Yes, Father," Sadie answered evenly. "But I have…"

Ruth snapped at Sadie, interrupting her. "You wicked girl, you keep quiet until your parents have heard the whole story."

Willing herself to remain quiet and still, Sadie took a deep breath and leaned back in the rocking chair. She would have to trust in her parents to give her a fair hearing at some point, but clearly there was no way to stop Ruth's fury. Best to let her say her piece and hope she would calm herself down.

John put his hand on his wife's arm to quiet her. "Samuel, your daughter has been writing about very worldly things. She has even written about some very wicked things. Did you know that she has helped gay men in your shop?

"I did not know that. Is that true, Sadie?"

"Yes, father."

"Why didn't you tell me?"

"I didn't think it was important."

Ruth stood from the loveseat. "See, Samuel. She condones homosexuality. She has been corrupted and I will not have her corrupt my son."

Sadie realized that she would have to stand up for herself. "I know that it is wrong to be gay. I believe that it is important to treat all of our customers with respect, though. Just because someone is different does not mean that I should throw them out of the store and refuse to do business with them."

"But it is wicked of you to waste your time writing about this sinful lifestyle," Ruth countered. "It is proud of you to think that you have the right to determine your own behavior."

Hannah took the opportunity to speak. "Ruth, we thank you for bringing the matter to our attention, and Samuel and I will speak to Sadie."

"Oh, but that is not all! To begin with, Sadie thinks far too highly of herself. Plain people do not go around showing off their writing. And to make things worse, Sadie has persuaded Abram to write in the journal as well. They have a record of their behavior, and they should be ashamed."

Sadie felt compelled to speak. "But Ruth, did you read what I wrote? I have done nothing wrong. I merely use the talents God has given me…"

"Talents? Talents??? Who are you to be so proud? You think that God wants you writing about gays and riding around with Nathan Kobel? You think God wants you drinking wine?"

"I tasted wine once. We tasted wine once. We were not drunk, and we did nothing wrong," Sadie said softly.

"Young lady, you have no right to tell me that you have done nothing wrong. I know what it is like to begin spending time with outsiders like Nathan Kobel. I know what it is like to believe that there is no harm in trying something a little new or different. The reason we live apart from the world is that you cannot be Plain in the world. We must be separate, and I will not have you tempt my son any longer."

Ruth stood up and gestured to her husband to join her. "Samuel and Hannah, it is up to you to decide what is to be done with Sadie. If you choose not to bring her behavior to the attention of the Bishop, we will take no action on your behalf. But we will not permit Abram to be ensnared in Sadie's sins. He will not see your daughter privately again."

John Byler stood and took the fabric-covered journal from Ruth's clutches, and he passed the book to Samuel. "You can decide what is to be done with this book. We will not have it in our house any longer. Be wary, Samuel, of the curiosity that lurks in your daughter's heart. She looks too fondly on the world. See that she isn't tempted beyond what she can bear."

Ruth insisted on getting in one last dig at the Zooks. "And you should examine your lives and the way you do business and see if you have not set the example for Sadie yourselves. There's not far to go between electric lights at home and children with cell phones and cars. Look in your own hearts and see your example for what it is. Ask yourself if you are really Plain." Ruth walked out of the room and out the door without another word or a look behind her. Stunned by Ruth's harsh and judgmental tone, Hannah and Samuel were speechless.

Sadie spoke up softly, startling John, almost as if he'd forgotten that she was in the room. "What did Abram say when you talked to him?" she asked.

"Sadie, Ruth and I will deal with Abram. He is no longer any of your concern."

John Byler followed Ruth out into the rain. The Byler children came out from the barn, joined their parents in the buggy, and rolled out of the yard. Standing in the open doorway, a few raindrops blowing in to dampen her face, Sadie watched them leave. She turned to her parents. "I want to explain."

Seated in the parlor once again, Samuel looked at the book in his hands. "Sadie, tell me about the book. What do you write about? Why have you hidden it?"

"Da, I have not sinned in writing it. I love to write, and I believe that writing is one of the ways that God has given me to keep my focus on Him and on being humble. I do write about Englishers because I interact with them in the store. I feel like I learn lessons about what it is to be Plain because of the customers in the store."

Hannah spoke up. "What was Ruth talking about with the wine?"

"Mama, Abram and I went to the lake with Nathan Kobel on Friday evening. He brought a girl with him, and she had packed a bottle of wine. I tasted it, and so did Abram. We just took a taste and we did not get drunk. I know that drunkenness is a sin, and I would not behave that way. We did nothing wrong. I have nothing to be dishonest about."

Samuel looked at Hannah and then back at his daughter. "Sadie, I have never know you to be dishonest, and I have never seen wickedness in you. I trust you."

Sadie let out a huge sigh. "Da, I will not disappoint you. In fact, if you want to read the journal, I will let you keep it."

Hannah took the book from Samuel and handed it to Sadie. "There is no need. I know your heart, and we trust you. I fear that Ruth Byler will cause you some trouble, though, Sadie. You may no longer be able to see Abram. We can't interfere with the way the Bylers raise their children."

"Mama, isn't there something we can do, though? She has falsely accused me, and she has no right to interfere with what Abram wants as long as he follows the *ordnung*."

"Sadie, you know we must respect their wishes. Abram must decide for himself how to handle John and Ruth's rules for him. He is a man grown, and he is a full member of the church. He will have to stand on his own for what he believes is right."

"I guess so, Mama." Sadie slumped in her chair as tears started to well in her eyes. "Maybe Abram will be able to make them understand that we have done nothing wrong," she said quietly, in a tone that suggested that she had little faith in that hope.

Hannah and Samuel quietly left the room, and Sadie was alone with her journal. She felt as though she'd lost a friend, and the only hope she had was that when she saw Abram in the morning at work, that the storm would have blown over. Surely God could see into her heart and know that her connection with Abram was free of sin and was pure and pleasing in His sight.

Chapter Fifteen

Sadie awoke on Monday morning with eyes swollen from her tears the night before. She'd finally fallen asleep later than usual, and only because she was emotionally spent, worn out from the tears and drama. Opening her swollen eyes, she was surprised to see that the sun had already risen. She couldn't remember ever having slept so late, and she figured that her parents must have let her sleep in as a kindness. Deciding to steal just a few more moments, Sadie opened her journal, water-stained now from Ruth's having kept it outside in the rain, and she wrote a few lines to Abram.

She wasn't sure if he would take the journal from her, and for that matter, she wasn't even sure if he would follow his parents' instructions and cut off all contact with her, but she knew for sure that the thought of losing Abram's friendship felt like a giant hole had opened in her life. She had to try to talk to him. She would just have to remind herself that she had not sinned, and neither had Abram. If they had done nothing wrong, then there was no good reason for them to stay apart – at least no reason that Sadie could see.

Making up her mind to be positive and approach the day with hope, Sadie got out of bed, washed her face, and dressed for the day. Greeting her mother and sisters who were in the kitchen putting finishing touches on breakfast, Sadie thanked them for the extra sleep. Promising to take care of the lion's share of the dishes, she carried plates into the dining room to set the table.

Breakfast over, dishes washed, and chores finished, Samuel and Sadie had a long talk on their way to work, talking about some of the topics that Sadie had written about.

"Da, I know that it is wrong to spend too much time thinking about the English and worrying about how they think about us, but I don't think that it's wrong to be polite to people who I believe lead sinful lives. After all, since they're not Plain, who am I to judge? Isn't that up to God?"

"Sadie, it's hard to say. While I do think there is a danger in spending too much time with those who aren't Plain, I can't say that I think it is wrong for you to treat them with respect. After all, Jesus found it in his heart to forgive sinners."

"And it would be different if someone in our church said they were gay, right?"

"Sadie, don't even say such a thing!" Samuel exclaimed.

"Da, I know it's wrong, but if it were someone Plain, then we would shun them. I understand, but it's different if it's an Englisher. They're not part of our community, and I don't see a good reason to be rude or to refuse to do business with them."

Samuel was silent for a good half-mile before he spoke again. "Sadie, I don't know that I agree with you, but I also don't know that I can find fault with your reasoning. Best not to talk about this anymore, though. If that is the sort of thing that is in your book, I can see why John and Ruth were so upset."

"I understand, Da."

"In fact, I think it's probably best to keep that book hidden, after all," Samuel said with a little sideways smile at his daughter.

When Sadie and Samuel pulled into the yard of Ephrata Woodworks, Sadie was pleased to see Abram's buggy outside the wood shop. As they pulled next to the buggy, though, she was surprised that Abram hadn't come out into the yard to help unhitch the horse form the Zook's buggy as usual. Samuel climbed out of the buggy, unhitched the horse, and gave Sadie a look that indicated that he was puzzled as well. Deciding that she really had no other option, Sadie picked up the lunch basket and descended from the buggy as well. She glanced at the door to the workshop and turned to head toward the store. She unlocked the door, entered, and leaned back against the door as it closed. Abram hadn't come out to greet them! What could that mean?

Deciding that it would do no good to fret about Abram's behavior, Sadie started her usual morning routine. She checked the answering machine for messages, taking notes as she listened to the calls from customers inquiring about deliveries and from prospective customers asking about prices. Just as Sadie was about to start returning the phone calls, the door opened, and Abram stuck his head inside.

Dropping the receiver with a clatter, Sadie rushed from behind the counter and stopped short, unsure of what she should say. She simply stared at Abram and waited for him to speak.

Shuffling his feet a bit, Abram was clearly apprehensive. He looked around the room, as if he dreaded making eye contact with Sadie, and when he finally did, he could barely hold her gaze. He looked down at his shoes, covered in sawdust, and finally spoke. "Sadie, I am so sorry."

Sadie looked at Abram and realized that he looked awful. His eyes were red, as if he hadn't had enough sleep, and his posture was that of a broken man. Taking a step toward him, Sadie finally spoke. "Are you okay? You don't look so good."

"Oh, Sadie, I'm just sick about what has happened. It's not enough that my parents are disappointed and angry at me, but because I was careless with your book, now you are in trouble as well."

"But Abram, I am fine," Sadie explained. "I talked to Da and Mama, and they understand that there is nothing wicked in my journal, and they know that you and I have done nothing wrong. I explained everything to them after your parents left yesterday."

Abram looked at Sadie as if she had sprouted another

head. "What did you say?" he asked, as if he hadn't heard her properly.

"Everything is okay. My parents understand, and they're not angry."

Abram walked over to one of the chairs in the shop and sat down heavily. "Sadie, how can that be? My parents are so angry that they can hardly stand to look at me. They have told me that I can't spend any time with you, and for some reason Mother is particularly upset about my having spent Friday evening with Nathan Kobel. She was so angry that she was shaking."

"Abram, I am sure they will just need some time. Did you try to explain that there's nothing sinful in the journal, and that we only had a sip of the wine?"

"You don't understand, Sadie. I never realized before, but my parents aren't like yours. Samuel and Hannah trust you. They know that you are good and humble. My parents assume that everyone is wicked. They find it easier to believe bad things than good things."

Sadie sat down in another of the chairs and she was quiet as she thought about what Abram had told her. She had always known that the Bylers were very strict, eschewing conveniences that other Plain people permitted. She had never really thought about the connection between a mistrust of technology and a mistrust of people in general. She hadn't really spent much time in the Bylers' house, but from Abram's description, it was a very different climate than the Zook household.

"So what will you do, Abram"

"I do not know. I am twenty-one years old. I could be

married and have a family of my own. I am a full member of the church, and what I want to do is tell my parents that I am responsible for my own behavior." Abram stood up and began pacing the floor while he talked. "But my whole life I've been taught to obey my parents. I've been told that they know what is best and that obedience to God and my parents is always right. Sadie, I just do not know what to do."

"I suppose that you are the only person who can make the decisions that need to be made."

"I'm just so torn. I love our conversations, whether they are in person or in your journal. I would miss you if I do what my parents want."

"And I would miss you, Abram."

"But maybe they are right. Maybe it is wrong and selfish to think too much about the world and the English. Have I sinned? Have the thoughts I have about you been tainted by my having spent too much time reading words that look outward into the world, rather than inward on our community?" Abram removed his straw hat and ran a hand though his hair. "I should get back to work. Samuel will be looking for me."

Sadie was stunned and disappointed that Abram was actually considering complying with his parents' rules. She looked at Abram as he turned to walk toward the door. "I wrote a few lines for you last night. If you would like to read them, I have the book with me today."

"I have some thinking to do, and I will let you know at lunch. Sadie, thank you for being patient with me. I know it is hard. If only God would give me a sign, let me know what is right, then this would not be so difficult."

Sadie rewarded Abram with a little smile that almost concealed her disappointment. He left the building, and tears began to well in her eyes. As Sadie blinked back a few tears, she hoped that God would send Abram a sign. If Abram knew for sure one way or another, Sadie could learn to live with it. Drying her tears and giving herself a little mental shake, Sadie told herself that it was time to get back to work. God had no patience for lazy girls who got too caught up in everyday drama.

Abram went back inside the workshop, and he breathed deeply. The smell of fresh cut wood always gave him a feeling of peace. He loved his work with Samuel, and Abram determined to get back to work and be productive. As he returned to working on the dovetail joints for the dresser drawer he was building, it occurred that perhaps Samuel might have some insight into Abram's troubles. Though Samuel and Abram usually worked in companionable silence, he decided that his dilemma warranted changing things up.

"Samuel?"

"Mmm?"

"You know the situation with Sadie and me."

"I do."

"Can I talk to you about it?"

"Of course."

"My father and mother are furious for a couple of reasons. First, they think that Sadie is too worldly and will be a bad influence on me. Mother even went so far as to tell me that she thought Sadie might end up leaving the church altogether."

Samuel was surprised to hear that Ruth thought so little of his daughter, but he stayed silent and let Abram continue.

"They think that she spends too much time thinking about Englishers, and they think that her writing is a sign of her pride. I understand why they may have thought that at first, because I thought the same thing when I first accidentally found Sadie's journal. After I read it, though, I knew that she was just using her God-given talents. She is a good girl, and she has helped me to be a better person in just the couple of weeks that we've spent time together."

Realizing that Abram had a lot on his mind, Samuel got a drink of water and sat on the table that he'd finished the Friday before.

Abram continued. "So Mother wants me to completely stop spending time with Sadie, and she also was angry that I'd gone to the lake with Nathan Kobel. Here is my problem, Samuel. I've been raised my whole life to be obedient to God and to my parents, but I think that they are wrong in this instance. Sadie and I have committed no sins, and I want to continue to see her. I don't want to disobey my parents, though."

Samuel sighed. "That is indeed a problem, Abram, and I can not tell you what you should do. You have always been obedient and faithful. You are a good son to John and Ruth. I believe that Sadie is a good girl as well, and I think that her heart is pure. What I cannot do is counsel you to disobey your parents. I am afraid I can offer little advice to you, except to pray and hope that God shows you what is right."

"That is what I said to Sadie just a few minutes ago. Maybe God will give me a sign! I want to do what is right, but I need help. I need God to show me the way."

"Pray on it, Abram. Pray on it, and get that dresser finished, son."

Abram gave Samuel a little smile and got back to work. Before the men knew it, Sadie was calling them for lunch. The three workers shared their lunch outdoors in the shade next to the workshop, and they discussed the work and delivery schedules for some upcoming large orders. When lunch was finished, Abram asked Samuel for a few moments to talk to Sadie.

Both still seated at the table, Abram reached across the table and placed his hand over Sadie's. He took a breath and spoke. "Sadie, I have prayed about my…our… situation. I believe in my heart that we have done and will do nothing wrong. I have asked God to send me a sign if I am wrong. Since I know that I will do whatever is right, I believe that He will show me the way."

"You are a good man," Sadie told Abram, relishing the weight of his hand on hers.

"I hope to be." Abram stood and helped Sadie stack dishes and clear the table. "I would love to take your journal with me when I leave. I have decided to read it before I get home and keep it tucked away in my buggy. I will not lie to my parents, but there is no need shove the book in their faces."

Sadie swung the lunch basket over her arm and

beamed at Abram. "I'll go get it right now." Practically skipping to the store, Sadie vanished inside and returned with the book in hand. She handed it to Abram. "I believe that you are doing the right thing. Trusting God to show you the way will keep you on the right path."

Surprised at the relief she felt, Sadie breezed through the rest of her day, pleased that she and Abram had come to an understanding. She felt a bit sorry for Abram, as she'd never realized quite how hard his parents were on him. While Sadie's parents were demanding, in terms of requiring proper behavior and expecting every single member of the family to work hard to maintain the household, Sadie had never known anything other than the nurturing support of Samuel and Hannah. Discipline didn't have to be harsh, but the Bylers didn't seem to work that way. Realizing that Abram's hard and judgmental nature that had been so abrasive a few weeks ago was simply a product of his environment, Sadie felt a wave of compassion for the young man she was increasingly fond of. He'd never been a part of a family that was as supportive as hers, and she felt sorry for what he had missed.

When it was time to close up the shop for the evening, Abram helped Sadie into her father's buggy and quietly told her that he looked forward to seeing her in the morning, and that he would bring her journal back to her. He wasn't sure if he'd be able to write in it, but he would bring it back nonetheless. Abram and Sadie made plans to meet after dinner the next evening to go for a walk from the Zook's house. Sadie gave his hand a quick squeeze before he released her, and she practically grinned from her seat in the buggy. After all of the trouble caused by Ruth Byler and Sadie's journal, it was a relief to have matters settled with Abram. Sadie felt happily at peace, knowing that Abram had made the decision he thought best, and that she was included in that decision.

Chapter Sixteen

Abram sat in his buggy at Ephrata Woodworks, having decided that he would be better off reading Sadie's journal there, rather than sneaking around at home. He hadn't exactly decided how he planned to handle his parents – whether he should keep quiet about his decision to continue seeing Sadie and hope that his parents didn't bring the subject up, or whether he should be honest and simply tell them that he was old enough to know God's will on his own. He figured that he could mull that over on the way home.

Opening the little water stained book, Abram flipped to the page on which Sadie had written that morning.

Yesterday's worship service was just what I needed. The sermons on simplicity and on using your talents made me think of this journal and the way that it keeps me focused – helps me reflect on my behavior on a daily basis and think through whether I have been humble and Plain in every way I can. I know it is not everyone's way, and I know that Ruth may not understand it, but I feel like it makes me more mindful and deliberate if I record the events and my thoughts throughout the day.

I never expected that I would share my journal with anyone, and certainly not with you, but sharing it has opened my eyes. Abram, you have shared your thoughts with me, and I respect your desire to live a humble and Plain life. I hope that somehow, even in the face of the troubles yesterday, we can keep getting to know one another better and that God will find a way to show your parents that we have done nothing wrong and that our intentions and our behavior have both been proper and right.

As I write this, I don't know if you will ever read it. I don't know whether you will follow your parents' commands and refuse to see me, or if you will somehow make them understand the truth. If we are parted by these troubles, I will be sorry, and I will miss your company.

Sadie's simple honesty stunned Abram. While he was wracked by indecision and worry over how his behavior would affect his parents and their relationship, Sadie always seemed to find a way to cut through to the heart of a matter. She saw things so clearly. Abram realized that he could learn a lot from Sadie, and that living as simply and as honestly as she did was part of what made her a happier person. Resolving to think about her words and reply to her journal entry in the morning, Abram started toward home.

As soon as Abram pulled his buggy up to the barn that faced his house, he could tell that something was wrong. The two cows that the Bylers kept were complaining from the barn, reminding their owners that it was past time for them to be milked. Abram quickly unhitched and watered his horse, noticing that John's largest buggy was missing from the barn, along with one of their horses.

Unable to comprehend why the younger boys hadn't started the chores outside, Abram hurried inside to find out what was going on. He opened the kitchen door and immediately heard the sound of Katie crying. "What is wrong, Katie?"

Tears streaking her face, Katie looked up at Abram. "Mother is sick. Father didn't tell me exactly what is wrong, because he said he wanted to wait and tell the whole family all together. I think it is something bad."

"Where is the buggy?"

"Joshua and little John went to go get Grandmother and Grandfather. Sarah is upstairs with Mother and Father."

Abram was worried, but as he had never been particularly comfortable expressing emotions, he looked down at Katie. "Katie, I am sure everything will be alright. In the meantime, the cows need to be milked. I will be outside if anyone needs me."

Abram walked outside as if he had been programmed, like a robot. He automatically began the process of milking the two uncomfortable cows, working without thinking for a second about what he was doing. Stunned and unwilling to think through all of the things that could be wrong with his mother, he tightened his control over his emotions and focused on getting the evening chores done. Before he realized it, the shadows began to lengthen as the sun slipped toward the horizon.

Realizing that he was hungry, and immediately feeling ashamed of such a self-centered thought, Abram heard the approach of a horse and buggy. Heading outside to deal with the horse, Abram couldn't decide if he wanted to hurry up and head inside to find out what was wrong with Ruth, or if he wanted to drag his chores out so that he could go on without knowing for a little while longer. Squaring his shoulders and determining to face his fears, Abram got the horse squared away and headed inside.

John's mother, Sarah had thought to bring some sandwiches, correctly guessing that her son's family might not have made time to prepare dinner. As Abram entered the kitchen, she laid a hand on his arm and told him to go wash up for a quick dinner. Abram did as he was told and was surprised to see his sister, Sarah, setting the table with eyes red from tears recently dried. He looked at her with a question in his eyes, and she shook her head.

"Let us eat first. An empty stomach doesn't make anything better, and those boys will be starving after working at the farm all day."

When dinner was on the table, everyone but John and Ruth, sat down to eat. Though their grandparents only lived about twelve miles away, Joseph and Sarah Byler belonged to a different church, and they usually saw their grandchildren about once a month, on one of the Sundays not reserved for worship.

Joshua and John filled Joseph in on the status of the crops and livestock at the Stoltzfos farm, while Katie, temporarily distracted, chattered about how the school year had ended the week before. The meal ended quickly, as it was simple sandwiches, potato salad, and fresh fruit. Sarah helped her granddaughters clear and wash the dishes, and Joshua went upstairs to fetch John and Ruth.

Everyone settled in the living room to wait. When John came downstairs, it was clear that he was upset and trying to keep control of his emotions. Ruth followed him down the steps. She looked as though she had aged twenty years. Her thin shoulders were hunched, and she looked as though she hadn't slept in days. She sat next to her husband. John, typically not demonstrative, wrapped his arm around Ruth's shoulders as she began to tear up.

Looking around the room at his family, Abram was terrified. His mother must be very sick to have worried everyone this much. As he looked at his sisters, he saw Sarah and Katie both begin to cry before their father even started to speak. Thinking about the medical history of Ruth's family, both her parents deceased many years ago, Abram knew for a certainty what was coming, and he would have given anything to prevent his father from having to speak the words that followed.

John tightened his hold on Ruth's shoulders and spoke. "Your mother has cancer." The room was silent, but for the quiet tears from Sarah and Katie. There was no expression of shock, as clearly everyone in the room had feared the worst, but guessed the outcome. John continued. "We went to see the doctor a few weeks ago, and they ran some tests. We didn't want to worry any of you until we knew for sure, but today we went to town, and it's certain. Ruth has cancer. She will need surgery, and then we will have to decide what further treatment she will need. It will not be easy, but we may be able to cure her completely."

"Does that mean that she may die?" Katie asked in a thin, wavering voice.

"It is possible, but we will get her the very best doctors and the very best treatment we can. Many people are diagnosed with cancer, are treated, and are cured. Some are not, and we have to prepare ourselves for that, while hoping and praying for the best."

Katie, sobbing, rushed across the room and buried her face in her mother's lap. Ruth put a hand on Katie's head and whispered to her daughter, and then she sat up a little straighter. "Children, God only gives us what we can bear. I want you to be strong and use these difficult days ahead to think about how God rewards those who follow his laws and how God will punish those who break his commandments." As Ruth finished speaking, her eyes were focused squarely on Abram.

Abram was taken aback that even in the face of being diagnosed with cancer, his mother still took that opportunity to exert her authority over him. As his family dried tears and went their own way from the living room, Abram continued to sit, unable to move as if he were weighed down by all of the world's troubles.

Abram sat straight up, electrified by the memory of the commitment he'd made earlier in the day. When he had prayed for God to send him a sign to let him know if he should defy or obey his parents, he never expected that he would get an answer so quickly, so clearly, and so terribly. Abram slumped over, head in his hands and completely devastated by the guilt he felt. Surely God had answered him. Surely his mother's cancer was a result of Abram's sins. He should never even have considered defying his parents. He had been taught obedience his whole life, and now that he'd finally dared to stand up for what he wanted, he had been shown that his desires were proud, unclean, and deadly.

Abram knew with certainty that his only option was to end his relationship with Sadie and obey his parents. Maybe, he thought, if he could be truly contrite, and if he could cleanse Sadie's influence from his mind and heart, maybe God would spare his mother. Maybe he could be good enough to make a difference.

Abram looked up as his mother came back into the living room. She looked tired, just completely emotionally worn out. She sat down in the chair next to Abram's.

"Abram, I hadn't ever planned on telling you this story, but I think there's something you need to hear.

There's a reason why I'm worried about your beginning a relationship with a young woman who is so interested in matters that shouldn't concern Plain people. You may think that I do not know anything about relationships between Plain folk and Englishers, but I have two stories to tell you. After you hear what I have to say, you will understand."

"Mother if you are too tired, or if you do not feel up to it, we can do this another time," Abram said softly. As angry as he had been with his parents earlier, that anger had melted in the face of his mother's illness.

"No, Abram. You are old enough to understand the reasons why your father and I are holding you to these rules. There's no easy way to begin this story. You have an uncle. One you've never met. His name was Joseph, and he was your father's younger brother." Ruth paused to let the information sink in before she continued. "He and your father were very close, but Joseph met a girl – an English girl – at one of the restaurants in Ephrata. She worked there as a waitress, and Joseph and John met her the same evening. Your father said she was smart and very proud. She wore lots of makeup and jewelry, and she didn't dress modestly. She had worked at the restaurant for a long time, and Joseph started going in just to see her. Sometimes your father was there, and sometimes Joseph went in by himself." Ruth sighed and leaned back in the chair.

"Mother, why did Father never tell me about his brother?"

"You will know soon enough. John feels guilty to

this day, because he knew that Joseph was going to see this English girl, and he suspected that they had gone on some dates. John did not tell their parents, and soon enough, the girl got into trouble, and Joseph had to marry her. Since she would never become Plain, Joseph chose this girl over everything he had known his whole life. He left the church, was shunned by everyone who had known him, and he has never been welcome back here. They moved somewhere in Florida, and you father has never seen his brother again. He still misses him, but you cannot be Plain if your wife is worldly. It will never work."

"Mother, I am sure that Father misses his brother, but that is not the same as what Sadie and I have. She is Plain. She is a good, modest, Plain girl, and she always will be."

"Abram, that is the problem, though. You do not know for sure that Sadie will always want to be Plain. What if she spends so much time dealing with Englishers that she decided that she wants a taste of their world? People do leave our community, and they almost never return. The world is too corrupting. It's like an infection, ruining and sickening everything it touches."

"Good grief, Mother. That's a bit of an exaggeration, isn't it?"

Ruth began to get a little agitated. "No, Abram. And that's the problem. You do not see how dangerous that girl can be. Joseph did not go into that restaurant believing that he would have to marry a pregnant waitress and leave all of his friends and family. But that is exactly what happened. You need to be more careful."

"Okay, Mother. I get your point."

"That's not all, Abram. There is another story, one that will be harder for me to tell you because it is about me. I am not proud of everything I have done in my life. I should have listened to my parents when I was younger, and now that they have both passed away, I have lost my chance to learn from them."

"Mother, you do not need to say any more."

"I do. I need to tell you this, so that you will understand how vigilant you need to be. You cannot let your guard down against the world, not even for a minute. Many years ago, before your father and I started courting, I was vain enough to think that I could resist any temptation. My parents were very faithful and strict, as your father and I are with you. My parents and I lived next to Andrew and Martha Kobel. You never met them, but Andrew Kobel died many years ago, and Martha lives in an old folks home in Lancaster. They had four sons, and the oldest was Benjamin. You know him because he's Nathan Kobel's father. Before Benjamin was married, though, he was a bit loose. He went to public school, with all of the other Mennonite boys, and he always had a string of pretty English girls he courted.

"I was very surprised one summer – he was in high school, and I was working with mother, baking pies and bread to sell at the market in town – and Benjamin took a shine to me. I would not pay him any attention at first. He was Mennonite, and I always knew that I would marry a

Plain man, not one of those proud men who think they can be pure and mix in with the world.

"But Benjamin was persistent, and he flattered me, and I enjoyed his attention. He could have had any girl he wanted, but he seemed to want me. I was even foolish enough to think that he might even want to marry me and that he might convert and become a member of our congregation. We courted for months, and I am embarrassed to admit that I let him take some liberties."

Abram winced, as he did not want to think about Ruth courting and some man having the same thoughts about Ruth as he had recently had for Sadie.

"I can confess this to you, Abram, because I was still pure when I married your father much later, and because I have confessed my sin to God and am forgiven for my sins. But while I was thinking about my wedding day, Benjamin was only thinking about his next conquest. He moved on to another girl, and left me behind, heartbroken and ashamed. I do not think that he knew that I believed myself in love with him, and I was foolish to have forgotten that it is not attraction or emotion that makes a marriage, but dedication and faith.

"He left me without a second thought, and I was embarrassed for having believed that he cared about me, and I was a fool for having been so proud to think that I could change him, that I could bring him to our way of life. I should have heeded my parents' warnings and let a Plain man court me. I thought I knew better than they did, and I was wrong."

Abram was silent. Though he was fond of Sadie, his

mother's tale, coupled with the fact that God had so clearly given him a sign, made him think that he would have to obey his parents, just as he had decided before his mother told him her stories.

Ruth realized that Abram understood her. "And Abram, you must be careful with that Nathan Kobel as well. He is sure to be just like his father, vain and proud, and careless with the feelings of others. He does not care about you, and he does not care if you are shunned by all of your family and friends. He is no friend to you."

Feeling assaulted by the news about his mother's cancer, and beaten down by Ruth's relentless insistence that he stop seeing Sadie and Nathan, Abram just gave up. "Mother, I will not see Sadie again. I will give her journal back, and I will not read any more of her writing. I will not spend time with Nathan either. I will do as you and Father have asked."

Ruth stood and began to leave the room. "We will not speak of your uncle or of my foolishness again. I will tell John that you have finally seen the truth in what we have told you."

Abram just sat in silence as Ruth walked out. He knew that there were hard times ahead for every member of his family. His mother was sick, and the operation she would need would be difficult and expensive. Abram knew that treatment for cancer made patients very sick and tired, and given what John had said earlier, there was a chance that even if they got Ruth the very best treatment that she still might not have very long to live. Ruth's cancer would cost his family dearly in energy, emotion, and financial resources as well. The Bylers didn't have health insurance and would be paying for the procedures as they occurred. They would certainly find the money, but it wouldn't necessarily be easy.

Indulging himself in a brief moment of self pity, Abram reflected on the cost that he would have to pay as well. Sadie had been a bright light in his life, recently discovered and barely explored. He would miss their thoughtful discussions. He would miss seeing her light up a room with a smile meant just for him. He would miss her sweet, humble nature and her laughter. Realizing that a relationship of a few weeks paled in comparison with Ruth's condition, Abram felt the loss nonetheless.

Abram didn't even want to think about telling Sadie that he couldn't continue to see her. Would she think that he was weak, caving in to his parents' demands? Would she understand that God had sent him the sign he'd asked for? Sadie had been so happy earlier that day when Abram had decided to defy his parents, and he expected that she would be equally disappointed when he changed his position. He would have to make her understand his reasons, though, and let God take care of the rest.

Afraid that he would have trouble expressing himself to Sadie in person, Abram decided that the best way to tell Sadie might be through the journal that started the whole relationship. He figured that his parents would understand if he wrote one more entry in the journal. Abram went outside to his buggy, retrieved the journal, and headed upstairs to bed. Face scrubbed clean, and weary to the bone, Abram crawled in bed and began to write by the light of the oil lamp next to his bed. Surprised to find that a tear landed on the page as he wrote, Abram wondered if Sadie would be able to tell that his sorrow had marked the page and blurred his words. Abram finished the journal entry, extinguished the lamp, said his prayers, and fell into a dreamless sleep.

Chapter Seventeen

Sadie awoke and hoped that the day would dawn as bright and cheerful as she felt. She looked forward to seeing Abram at work, and she had their evening walk to look forward to as well. Sadie loved the early summer, before the oppressive heat and humidity set in. June evenings were lovely, and she relished the thought of strolling through Lancaster County's rolling green hills with Abram.

"My goodness, Sadie. You look like a happy girl this morning," Hannah greeted her daughter as Sadie entered the kitchen.

"Yes, Mama. I talked to Abram yesterday, and everything is going to be okay. He is coming over this evening to take me for a walk after dinner. If I get some extra weeding done in the garden this morning, can I go?"

"Of course, Sadie. The garden is in pretty good shape, and if you neaten it up this morning, I'll have plenty of help this evening cleaning up after dinner. God gave us these beautiful summer evenings. You should enjoy them."

Sadie and Hannah made cinnamon rolls together and set them aside to rise before breakfast. They had just finished slicing ham to heat for the morning meal when Esther and Miriam arrived in the kitchen. Esther's long hair was loose, and she carried her prayer covering.

"Mama, will you braid my hair for me?" the young girl asked. "When Miriam does it, it's always too tight."

Hannah sat in one of the kitchen chairs and took the hairbrush from Miriam. "Miriam, if you'll peel and slice potatoes, Sadie is going to work in the garden for a bit before breakfast." While Hannah spoke, she brushed Esther's long dark gold hair. She quickly braided it and twisted it into a bun, fastening the bun with bobby pins that Esther handed her. It took almost no time to put the girl's hair up, as Hannah had a lifetime of experience with neatly concealing long hair. Hannah fastened the prayer covering with pins and sent Esther out to help Sadie in the garden.

The girls weeded the strawberry patch and picked a basket full of sweet, ripe berries. Sadie cut the last of the season's asparagus and helped Esther with reciting her multiplication tables while Ester weeded around the tomato plants that seemed to have grown several inches overnight. Sadie loved working in the garden, and she knew that she would be glad of the strawberry preserves that Hannah would make that day – happy for a taste of June year-round.

When the girls heard the bell ring, they knew that

breakfast would be on the table soon. They washed their hands at the pump in the yard and were joined by their brothers and father. As they trooped inside, Sadie could smell the fresh baked cinnamon rolls that were her favorites. Miriam was pouring glasses of milk at the table, and everyone sat and readied themselves for prayers.

When the silent prayers were over, plates were filled and food was passed. Miriam and Hannah talked over their goals for the day, strawberry preserves being at the top of the list. Since Miriam and Esther were home from school for the summer, Esther asked if she could play with the Kobel girls that afternoon.

Isaac, youngest of the boys and Esther's favorite brother mournfully shook his head and looked at Esther with sad eyes. "Esther, the Kobel girls have said that they don't want to play with little girls with grasshoppers in their hair."

Esther predictably turned into a little tornado of twisting and brushing off of imaginary insects. Hannah calmly shut down Isaac's joking with the glare than only mothers can give, and after Isaac finally convinced Esther that there weren't any bugs in her hair, the family could return to enjoying their meal.

Young Samuel waited for Esther to calm down, and he addressed Sadie. "Luke Stoltzfos told me that he saw John and Ruth Byler at the doctor's office yesterday. He said that it looked like Ruth was crying." Samuel knew, of course, that there had been some controversy involving the Bylers and Sadie, though he didn't know the details. "Do you know what is going on?"

"I do not know," Sadie answered. "Abram didn't say anything about it, but after Sunday, I am not sure that he would."

Though Sadie's siblings were curious about the conversations that had occurred in the parlor, none of them was planning to ask. In such a big and close family, sometimes you had to let people keep their secrets.

Sadie looked at young Samuel. "Did Luke say what doctor's office they were visiting?"

"No, he didn't say. I can ask him if you like."

"No, no need to pry. If it is any of my business, Abram will tell me. I do hope everything is okay, even though Ruth has not been very charitable"

"Sadie," admonished Hannah. "Let us not criticize our sisters."

Bowing her head, Sadie signaled her acknowledgement of Hannah's gentle criticism. Putting negative thoughts aside, Sadie finished her breakfast and helped her sisters and mother with the cleanup.

Even though Sadie knew that it was foolish to wish one's life away, she wished she could skip ahead to her arrival at work, when she would get to see Abram. She was still surprised at how much she looked forward to seeing Abram – the young man she'd always thought of as gruff and stern. The discovery that he was more open and warm than she'd ever guessed was such a delight. Thanking God for the gift of Abram, Sadie climbed into the buggy for the trip to work.

Both Samuel and Sadie were surprised that by the time they arrived at Ephrata Woodworking, Abram had not yet arrived. The young man always arrived before they did, and when Sadie didn't see his buggy, she was filled with a sense of foreboding. She knew for certain that something was wrong, and she hoped that it was something simple – perhaps a summer cold had kept Abram home, or perhaps he'd needed to help his father with a job at home.

Sadie couldn't help but think, though, that Abram's having left work the night before with the intention of defying his parents might have something to do with his absence. What if Abram had argued with John and Ruth? What if they had shunned him and forced him to leave the house? There were too many terrible possibilities to contemplate, and Sadie closed her eyes, said a quick prayer for peace and patience, and descended from the buggy.

Knowing that she would see Abram's buggy as soon as he arrived – if he arrived, Sadie headed into the store to get to work, hoping that she could distract herself. Sadie was surprised to have several early morning customers in the store, and a sweet young couple expecting their first child was asking about the different kinds of wood that could be used for rocking chairs when Sadie saw Abram's buggy pull into the yard. Sadie tried so hard to keep her focus on answering the customers' questions as she watched Abram through the window. Assuming that he would see the car parked outside the store and understand that she was busy, Sadie resolved to find the first chance she could to talk to Abram.

Sadie finished writing up the couple's order for a

hickory rocking chair and an oak dresser, and she promised to call the couple when the furniture was finished. The very moment that the couple's car left the lot, Sadie saw the door to the workshop open and Abram head her way. His stride was even and determined; he moved with a purpose. Sadie brightened at his approach, and when the door to the store opened, she wore a bright smile.

"Good morning, Abram! I was worried when I didn't see your buggy here. What happened to delay you?"

Abram stepped inside and closed the door behind him. "Sadie, we have to talk. Can you spare a few minutes for me?"

"Silly man, of course I can. I'm always happy to talk to you."

"Sadie, you will not be happy when you hear what I have to say. This is difficult for me, though, so I hope you will let me say my piece."

Sadie's face fell as she realized that Abram was upset, barely able to keep his emotions under control. She sat in one of the chairs around a dining room table, and Abram joined her, sitting across from her.

Abram put his hands flat on the table, took a deep breath and began what was one of the most difficult conversations he'd ever had. "Sadie, I asked God yesterday for a sign. I believed that our relationship was good and right, and I knew in my heart that if God approved, that I would know it. I wanted nothing more than for God to show me what was right."

Abram stopped talking and looked at Sadie. Her blue eyes wide, she sat quietly and waited for him to continue.

"God answered my prayers, and even though I do not like the answer I received, I must obey. Sadie, God has given me a sign that I must obey my parents, and I can not see you any longer."

No longer able to control herself, Sadie had to speak up. "But Abram, just yesterday, you believed that we were right to continue getting to know one another better, that we had done nothing wrong. How can you possibly have changed your mind overnight?"

Abram sighed. He had known that Sadie wouldn't understand, that it wouldn't make sense to her unless he showed her the truth. "Sadie, I didn't change my mind. God changed my mind. You have to know that I wouldn't be telling you this if I weren't sure."

Sadie's voice trembled as she spoke. "I will listen."

"I left here yesterday believing that I was right. When I arrived home last night, everything changed." Abram sat up straighter and looked at Sadie's hands resting on the table across from him. He wanted nothing more than to cover her hands with his own, but that would not make things any easier. If he intended to end their relationship, he might as well start right away.

"Sadie, my mother is sick. Very sick. She has cancer."

"Oh, Abram, I am so sorry," Sadie exclaimed, her hand moving to cover her mouth in shock.

"She will have surgery and whatever treatment the doctors recommend, but both of her parents passed away from cancer, and we do not know for sure if God will cure her." Abram stopped speaking, bowed his head, and Sadie's heart melted as she saw a few teardrops fall to the surface of the table. Abram wiped his eyes and continued. "We do not know the future that God has in store for her, but I do know one thing. Mother's illness is a sign. It is not the sign that I wanted, but it is the sign that I asked for."

Sadie had to protest. "Abram, you can not possibly believe that Ruth's illness has anything to do with our relationship. God would never be so cruel!"

Frustrated, Abram pushed back his chair and stood up to pace. "Sadie, I am certain. Please do not make this more difficult for me. Not only do I have my mother's illness on my conscience, but now I have to explain to you? I know that God will only give us the troubles that we can handle, but this is almost more than I can bear!"

"I do not want to make this harder for you, but you have to understand why I am upset. I have come to care for you, Abram, and now you tell me that I must stop?"

"Sadie, you must do as your heart tells you. I suggest that you pray for guidance, as I have. I am doing a terrible job of explaining myself, I'm afraid." Abram stopped pacing. "Let me go get your journal. I wrote one last entry to you, and I hope that it will explain better than I have managed to."

Sadie just sat at the table, stunned by the radical change in the way she had expected this day to go. She didn't know what to think. She was devastated for Abram that his mother was so sick. Thinking about how she would feel if it were Hannah who faced such a horrible disease, Sadie imagined that she might not have had the strength to get out of bed that morning. She knew Abram was hurt and anxious, but Sadie also thought that perhaps he wasn't seeing God's whole plan. She knew, with every part of her being, that God would never have used Ruth's cancer to punish Abram.

Abram came back inside with Sadie's journal. He crossed the room, placed the volume on the table, and looked into Sadie's eyes. "I am sorry Sadie. I should have trusted my instincts when I first found your journal, and now, because of my poor judgment, my mother has to pay the price. I will miss you, and I am sorry."

Without another word, Abram left the building to return to work. Sadie watched him cross the yard, and she felt as if her heart was breaking. She didn't even realize that she was crying until she saw that her tears had landed on the cover of her journal. Thinking that there was nothing that a few lines of Abram's writing could do to heal her hurt, she opened the book anyway. She was surprised to see a longer entry from Abram than he'd ever written before.

Chapter Eighteen

Sadie, I think that I have nothing to lose at this point. I will be completely honest with you. You are unlike any other girl woman I have ever met. You have challenged me. You have made me think. You have made me question things I never had before. You have stirred feelings and desire in me that I have never felt. Next to you, every other woman I have met is flat and uninteresting. I can't believe that I am going to write this, but Sadie, you are the only woman I have ever met that I want to spend the rest of my life with.

But you and I (and everyone else in our community) know that desire and feelings aren't the foundation of a strong marriage. God is.

The last few weeks that I have spent with you will be hard — if not impossible — for me to put out of my mind. I will remember them for the rest of my life. But Sadie, we aren't put here to follow our own selfish desires. We are put here to do the work that needs to be done, to follow God's plan for us, and to strengthen our community. I see now that my parents were right. My involvement with you has been selfish, and would eventually be destructive.

Passion cannot last. God expects us to sacrifice our selfish and immature desire for passion, and that is what I will do. It breaks my heart, but I will do as my parents have commanded. I will do whatever needs to be done to help my mother fight this terrible illness. I will try to be a better son and hope that I can atone for my sins.

Though I will miss you for the rest of my life, I am thankful that God showed me the sign that I needed to change my course before I could make a decision that would be permanent. I hope that you will respect my decision and let me grieve in peace.

Sadie, I also hope that you will take some advice from me – as a friend and a brother in the church. Be careful. You need to look inward – to your heart and to our community, rather than outward toward the world. There is nothing but sin and heartache for you there. Though I have indulged in this selfish writing with you, I will do it no longer, and if I happen to find another one of your journals again, I will have to give it to Bishop King and let him decide your fate. If you continue to write, I cannot continue to keep your secrets.

Sadie, some small part of me hopes that I am wrong, though I know it is sinful to say so. Like the decision I made before, though, I know that God will make my path clear to me if I am open to His guidance. I believe that I am doing the right thing in ending our relationship before it goes any further, but if I'm wrong, I will look for God to correct me.

Please respect my decision.

I wish you well.

Abram

Sadie ran her fingers over Abram's signature, and then she reread Abram's entry. She closed the book thoughtfully and decided that she couldn't even begin to sort through all of the conflicting feelings and thoughts that filled her head. Part of her wanted to march across the yard and shake Abram until he realized that he was being a fool. Another part of her was heartbroken that she was about to lose the surprisingly sensitive man who had just penned such a heartbreaking confession to her. Part of her was angry, part hurt, and part just baffled.

Realizing that she could easily lose herself for hours in the maelstrom of thoughts that occupied her, Sadie stood up from the table, briskly hid her journal in its usual spot behind the counter, and snatched up the pile of outgoing mail on the shelf. She scribbled a note instructing any shoppers to visit the woodshop, locked the door, and started the walk to the post office. Though she didn't need stamps, and could have just put the letters in the mailbox, Sadie simply had to get outside and clear her head.

The post office was about a mile away, the perfect distance to get some fresh air and mull things over. Sadie knew that she really had no choice but to respect Abram's decision. She couldn't very well haunt his steps and plead with him to change his mind. It wouldn't be proper for a woman to challenge a man's decision, and Sadie knew that her parents would be unwilling to support such a direct challenge to Ruth and John Byler, particularly in the face of Ruth's illness.

Feeling uncharacteristically frustrated, Sadie walked briskly, trying to make sense of everything that had happened in the last few days. As she walked, she managed to calm her thoughts a bit, and by taking some deep breaths, she started to feel a little more in control of her emotions. By the time Sadie got to the post office, she hadn't solved all of her problems, but she knew that should would find a way, with God's help, to do what was right.

Just as Sadie opened the door, she heard a woman's voice call her name from across the street. She turned, surprised, and saw Meredith waving at her. Meredith waited for a car to pass and dashed across the street. Sadie watched the girl – shoulder-length brown hair in two pigtails, white strappy tank, short navy skirt and sandals – as she approached.

Meredith, slightly out of breath from her sprint,

seemed happy to see Sadie. "Hey there! Good to see you again. How are you?"

Sadie, not accustomed to idle, polite conversation, answered honestly. "Truly, I am not doing so well. I have gotten some unwelcome news, and I am a little saddened. I am sure I will be fine, but it will take me a little while to adjust."

Meredith was clearly a little surprised by Sadie's candor. "Oh, honey, I'm sorry to hear that. Wanna go get some ice cream and tell me about it?"

"I probably should get right back to work, but as long as I'm quick I suppose it will be okay."

The girls walked a few doors up from the post office, ordered ice cream, and sat at a shaded picnic table. Sadie was a little surprised at herself for having agreed to something so frivolous, but she figured that her father and Abram could handle the business for a few minutes, and if Abram had to answer some questions about her absence, then so be it.

"So tell me what's wrong," Meredith prompted.

"Well, it may be hard for you to understand, since you aren't Plain, but I will try to explain. Abram has decided not to see me anymore. His parents believe that I'm wicked and worldly, and they have convinced him to agree to end things."

"But clearly they must have some reason, right?" Meredith asked, perplexed. "I mean, do they think you've done something wrong?"

"I keep a journal. That may not seem like a big thing to you, but Plain people don't do it. I have prayed and believe that I am not committing a sin, but Abram's mother and father do not see it that way. They believe that I am corrupting their son."

"Just for a journal? That's ridiculous!"

Sadie thought about trying to explain further and decided just to move on. "In any case, Abram asked for a sign from God to show him what he should do, and he believes that he has gotten that sign. His mother is sick. She has cancer, and he thinks that it is a sign from God that our relationship is sinful, and that he must end it."

"Oh, Sadie. I don't know what to say. I'm so sorry for Abram, but that doesn't make sense to me. Am I missing something here? How can cancer be a sign from God?"

Sadie sighed and took a bite of her ice cream as she considered her answer. "We do believe that God can act in our lives, that he can give us signs and direction for how we should behave."

"Right. But cancer?"

"Meredith, I do not know, but I do not believe that Ruth is sick because I wrote a journal and persuaded Abram to do it too. I do not understand everything about medicine, but would she not have had cancer for some time before any of this happened? Abram and I have only been spending time together for a few weeks!"

Meredith set her cup of ice cream down and looked at Sadie. "My mother is a doctor – not an oncologist, but she has patients who have cancer, and Abram's mother has had cancer cells growing for months, or even years. I don't know exactly what you believe, but there's no way that she has cancer because of you."

"What we believe does not always make sense to outsiders, but in this case I think that you are right. I do not blame Abram, exactly, as it can sometimes be hard to determine what God is trying to show you. I wish I could talk to him about it, but he has asked me to respect his decision, and I feel that I must give him the space he asks for."

"So wait! He gets to tell you all of this about his sign from God, and you have to take it and don't even get to discuss it?"

Sadie thought and realized that relationships must be much more complicated among the English. "It is our way to respect the Godly decisions of others. We do not have to discuss and analyze everything all the time. It is a simpler way."

Meredith contemplated Sadie's position. "I guess," she said, still unsure. "It just doesn't seem very fair to me."

Sadie gave her a weak smile. "That is the root of the problem, Meredith. We accept that life is not always fair. Being Plain is not about making things fair or even. Being Plain is about living the way God instructs, following His commandments, and putting the needs of our community before the selfish desires of any one person."

Shaking her head, Meredith took another bite of ice cream before she replied. "I guess I get it, but it just seems like it's gotta be hard sometimes, to try to always be unselfish."

"Yes. And this is one of those times."

Sadie and Meredith finished their ice cream in silence, enjoying the last few bites. When they'd finished,

Meredith moved as if to give Sadie a hug. Sensing the Amish girl's discomfort, Meredith backed off and settled for putting her hand on Sadie's arm instead.

"Sadie, it was good to see you, and I hope you and Abram can work things out."

"I thank you for lending an ear, Meredith. And thank you for the ice cream."

Sadie turned to leave without another word. Her walk back to the store was much slower as she thought over everything she and Meredith had talked about. She smiled as she realized that talking to the English girl had been a little like writing in her journal – Sadie gained some perspective and was able to focus better on what was right. She realized that she would have to give Abram the space he requested. To focus on her insignificant little relationship would cause strife in the congregation, and that would be a great wrong.

Realizing that she still felt sad, and that she would miss Abram for some time to come, Sadie still felt some peace. She knew that she had to do what was right for her community. She also knew that she could still, in good conscience, take refuge in her journal. All of the feelings that she had to conceal, and all of her frustration could find its voice in her little cloth bound book. Sadie knew that if she were perfect that she would not even feel frustrated or angry, but since she was imperfect, she believed that the journal was her best option for working through her feelings until she had better control of them.

Sadie got back to the store and found her sign missing and the door unlocked. Her heart leapt as she hoped that perhaps Abram had miraculously changed his mind and come inside to tell her. She opened the door, heart in her throat, and saw her father behind the counter, reading glasses on his nose, writing up a sales ticket.

"There you are, Sadie. Are you okay? I was worried."

Sadie nodded at her father. "I am sorry to have worried you, Da. I had a talk with Abram that upset me, and I needed some fresh air. I'm sorry you were disturbed in your work."

"It was no trouble. It is good for me to work with the customers from time to time, instead of working only with the wood." Samuel put down his pen and removed his glasses. "Is everything alright between you and Abram?"

Sadie sighed and tried to decide how to answer. "Things are not alright, but I am sure God has a plan. Abram has decided not to court me any longer, and he believes that God frowns on our relationship."

"And you? What do you think, Sadie?"

"I am hopeful that God will give Abram a sign that helps him see otherwise. But that is in God's hands. All I can do is put my trust in God that He will work it all out according to his plan."

Samuel looked at his daughter and was silently very proud of her, knowing that she had the strength and humility to do God's will. He nodded at her and crossed the room. When he reached the door, Samuel turned to Sadie. "You are a good girl, Sadie Zook." He walked outside and gently closed the door behind him.

Sadie looked over the ticket her father had written

up, corrected a small error, and neatly filed the paper. Scanning the room and seeing nothing that required her immediate attention, she retrieved her journal. As she began to write about the day's disappointing events, she hoped that some day soon God would fill her life and her journal with happier days.

"Trust in the LORD with all thine heart;
and lean not unto thine own understanding."

Proverbs 3:5

The Diary

Part 3 of 3

A Lines From Lancaster County Saga

Plain Love

Rachel Bauer

An Amish Christian Romance

Chapter Nineteen

Abram Byler looked around the waiting room, thinking about how different it was from the places he typically spent his days. Rather than painstakingly handmade wooden furniture, the room was furnished with sleek, black matte metal furniture with gray leather accents. The fluorescent lamps hummed softly behind their shiny chrome and frosted glass shades. Given that Abram was waiting for his mother and father to emerge from their post-op consultation with Ruth Byler's oncologist, and given the cold, impersonal feel of the room, Abram really could not have felt less comfortable.

As the outside door to the waiting room opened, Abram was glad to see his sister Sarah, older than her by a single year, return to the room. Sarah shared a tight, nervous smile with Abram as she sat down next to him.

"Are you warmer now?" he asked Sarah.

Sarah had stepped outside into the warm September sun to warm up while they waited for their parents, and she wrapped her arms around herself, the long sleeves little help against the over air conditioned office. "Better, at least for a little while. It is so lovely outside, I don't know why they keep it so cold in here."

Too uncomfortable for small talk, Abram nodded to his sister and returned his attention to the flat screen television mounted in the corner of the room. He was surprised to see a bible verse appear on the screen. Television was a novelty, of course, and Abram was riveted when the verse from Psalms appeared. "Delight yourself in the LORD and he will give you the desires of your heart."

The advertisement for the Christian dating website intrigued Abram, and he looked sideways to see if Sarah was watching it as well. He would never use a dating website – the absence of a computer and electricity would prevent it anyway, but the notion of using such an approach to finding a wife just puzzled Abram. Even though the ad mentioned God a lot, Abram had been raised to believe that marriages weren't built on attraction or on balancing family, work, and church. To the strict and devout Amish siblings in the waiting room, the ad just looked silly, and Abram thought that if people spent as much time working on their soul as they did on their appearance, that the divorce rate would be lower.

As Abram sighed and continued to wait, he thought about the verse from Psalms, though. He knew that it was neither humble nor Plain to focus his energy on his own selfish desires, but with no work to occupy his hands, Abram was unable to keep his thoughts from turning to the only woman that he had ever truly desired. Abram thought about her flashing blue eyes, her sweet cinnamon scent, and her lovely, long blonde hair that he would never see unbound and loose. Sadie Zook haunted his thoughts and dreams, regardless of the discipline he tried to exercise.

Abram knew that some day God would give him a wife, and Abram would be a good, hard working, faithful husband. What Abram did not know was if he would ever feel the intoxicating combination of desire, admiration, and pleasure that he had found in his brief and ill-fated relationship with Sadie. Hard as he tried to put thoughts of Sadie out of his mind, Abram found countless reminders every day that brought her sweet, honest face to mind.

Frustrated that even the passage of three months and his mother's illness could not extinguish the flame that kindled each time he thought of Sadie, Abram stood from his chair to stretch his broad shoulders and pace the waiting room floor. Sarah watched her brother begin to pace and checked the clock on the wall.

"I expect that they will be finished shortly," she told her brother. "I hope that the news is good."

Abram merely nodded in response as he shifted his thoughts back to where they belonged. God had sent Ruth's cancer to test not just her, but also the whole family, and though the road hadn't been easy, it showed no immediate sign of improvement. Ruth's surgery had been performed several weeks ago, and this consultation was to review her scans and plot a course of treatment to ensure that she had the best possible chance to survive.

"I cannot help but think that the longer it takes, the worse the news will be," Abram remarked.

Sarah looked up at her tall, strong brother who somehow seemed too large for the room they occupied. "Oh, stop, Abram. God will take care of Mother, and we must be positive for her sake. She has faced her cancer so bravely that we must try to do the same."

"You are right, Sarah. I am sorry. It is hard to be hopeful and trust in God at times like this."

Sarah reached up and took Abram's calloused, work-hardened hand. "And it is times like this one when it is the most important to have faith."

Abram sat back down next his sister. "Maybe some day God will show me how to have as much faith as you have, Sarah."

When the door from the doctor's office opened, both Abram and Sarah stood and waited for their parents to appear. One look at John and Ruth's faces told the story – the news had not been good.

John crossed the room to his children. "Let us go. We will explain what the doctor said on the ride home."

The Bylers left the office and Abram helped Ruth into the buggy that waited in the far corner of the parking lot, the horse tied beneath a nearby shade tree. John hitched the horse to the buggy, and the family began the journey from the center of Ephrata to their home roughly twelve miles away. Though Abram and Sarah were curious, they allowed their father to navigate the busy traffic and get to the main road that they would take to return home.

Once John had safely gotten the buggy to an easier

road to travel, he took a deep breath and addressed his children. "The doctor is fairly certain that the surgery got all of the cancer, but the kind of cancer that your mother has nearly always returns. It is very hard to cure."

Sarah's mouth fell open. "But he is going to do the radiation, right? And chemotherapy?"

"He recommends it. He recommends both, but they will both make Ruth very tired and very sick, and it is not certain that it will prevent the cancer from ever coming back. We have some decisions to make as a family."

Sarah spoke up again, and Abram decided that he would let Sarah conduct all of the questioning. Since the conflicts of a few months ago, Abram and his parents had felt a strain in their relationship.

"Is there nothing else that can be done, then? There has to be something they can do to cure her," Sarah insisted.

Ruth finally spoke from the front of the buggy. "There are some experimental drugs that they could try, and there is a new radiation treatment that might have some success, but Doctor Koch does not have experience with either of them. It will be expensive enough to go through the regular treatments, and even more dear if we have to find a fancy specialist who knows all of the new methods." Ruth's tone left little room for disagreement, implying that spending money on anything untested would be wasteful.

"But Mother, Abram and I both work, and we will help with the cost!"

John turned his attention from the road for a moment

as he turned to look at his children. "Your help is appreciated, and we have decided nothing. Ruth and I will pray and hope that God will show us what he would have us do."

Abram finally spoke from the back of the buggy. "Mother, I will help in any way I can. Sarah and I can take care of chores at home if you and Father are in town, and I can talk to Nathan Kobel if you need a ride to see a specialist."

Ruth's head whipped around at the mention of Nathan's name. "We do not need help from the likes of the Kobels." Lips pursed and jaw set, Ruth faced front again, and Abram recalled her long-standing animosity toward the Kobels.

Abram also knew that Sarah didn't know the story of Ruth's decades ago infatuation with Nathan's father, Benjamin, and his rejection of the Plain girl who had loved him enough to consider leaving the Amish faith. Ruth had finally realized that Benjamin was loose and flirtatious, and that the relationship in which she set such great store was nothing but a whim for Benjamin. Ruth had been steeped in her bitterness all these years, and Abram thought that she would live the rest of her life that way.

"I will find transportation from someone else, then, but we will do whatever we can to help you get better."

Softening a bit, Ruth glanced back at Abram. "Thank you," she said, as if those two polite words were all she could muster.

The rest of the ride home was pretty quiet, the only

noise from the horse's hooves and the impatient drivers who swung into the other lane to pass the slow horse and buggy. When they neared their home, Abram spoke up from the back of the buggy.

"What will we do?" he asked simply.

Without turning around, John answered his son. "We will pray for guidance from the Lord, and we will do what He wills us to do. Maybe we will have a sign from God."

No one else spoke as they pulled into their yard, near the barn. Joshua came out of the barn to help his father with the horse, and Sarah and Ruth went inside to begin preparing dinner. The men did the evening chores, milking their cows, cleaning up in the barn, and getting horses taken care of for the evening. The chores in the barn finished, Abram decided to step outside for a few quiet moments to himself before dinner.

He walked to the fence that marked the border of his family's property and rested his arms on the top section of the fence, still bright white since Abram had painted it only a few months before. As Abram looked out over the rolling hills, fields, and woods in the distance, he reflected on the last few months. Though it wasn't his nature to spend an inordinate amount of energy on introspection, Ruth's illness, combined with his struggles to be a good person, had altered his outlook.

Far in the distance, Abram saw one of his neighbors using the last of the sunny, late September day to bale hay, the machinery moving slowly and leaving behind a fresh-cut field full of square hay bales. Though Abram knew that his only thoughts should be about his mother and his duties to his family, Abram realized that he had just decided that the color of the hay was just slightly lighter than the color of Sadie Zook's hair.

Abram's thoughts flew from the Byler's land to settle near Sadie. In his mind, Sadie would be indoors now, in the half light of the Zook's dining room, perhaps setting the table for her family's dinner. Perhaps she hadn't yet turned on the electric lights and the sun, low on the horizon might illuminate her face as she worked. Abram knew every line in the picture – from the apron strings tied at her waist, to the stray tendrils of blonde hair that had worked loose from her prayer cap.

Maybe Sadie worked with Esther, laughing and instructing her little sister in the easy, affectionate way that seemed so pervasive and welcoming in Sadie's family. Abram wondered, as he imagined how Sadie might be spending that very moment, if she thought of him often. He wondered if she missed him as much as he did her. Not only did Abram miss her smiles, her clear, blue eyes, and her humble, sweet good heart, but he also missed her fresh and simple approach to her everyday life. Only Sadie could manage to look at her interactions with everyone – even the English – and find a way to emerge an even better person.

Abram felt disgusted with himself. How could he be fantasizing about Sadie now, of all times. Not only had he ended the brief relationship they'd shared, but he'd ended it because he believed that God had given him a sign that Sadie wasn't part of God's plan for Abram's life. Abram had been so sure that his parents were right – that

Sadie would be a negative influence on his life – that he'd regretfully, but decisively ended what had been the most fulfilling relationship he'd ever had, despite its brevity. Abram had prayed and decided that he would refuse to allow his selfish desires to encourage behavior that he believed was wrong. He would not defy his parents to satisfy his hopes for happiness.

How could he stand here and mope over Sadie when his mother needed his support? When the family faced such difficult – literally life and death – decisions? Abram had thought that since he'd acted in accordance with God's will that it would be easier to forget about Sadie. Forget about her honey-colored hair, sense of humor, and the sprinkling of freckles on her nose. He had been wrong.

Sadie haunted him. Not only did he have to see her at work every day, but she wouldn't leave his thoughts. He would think about her journal, the private writing in which she mulled over the events of the day and still managed, even with all of her contact with the English, to emerge as the sweet, humble, Plain girl that she was. How Sadie could think about the world as much as she did, while still remaining Plain was something of a mystery to Abram, and it was certainly something Abram's parents would never understand. It was also part of her charm.

Enough, Abram told himself. Enough.

He needed to tackle this problem of Ruth's illness – do everything that he could to help his family in this difficult time. And when Ruth was well again, Abram needed to find a wife. Twenty-one, nearly twenty-two was old enough. There had to be a girl who would suit God's plans for his life. After all, wanting to be excited by a girl, wanting to have her challenge his thoughts, have witty and interesting conversation – these things paled in comparison with the sober, hardworking life God expected. Right?

Gripping the top rail of the fence firmly, Abram turned from the early autumn scene before him, resolved to be stronger, more vigilant against these flights of fancy about Sadie. If he had to work himself harder so that he had no energy to spare for blonde girls, then work would be his refuge. Glad to hear the dinner bell, Abram turned to go inside, telling himself that he wouldn't miss the free and warm conversation that Sadie's family shared, but was sorely lacking in the Byler household.

Dinner was a predictably sober and quiet affair, and Abram was glad when it was over. Planning to retire early for the night and get a good night's sleep, Abram headed upstairs with his Bible. Abram made a list of the things he needed to pick up at the hardware store in the morning, and he settled in to read a few of his favorite passages.

Chapter Twenty

Sadie bounded out of bed early, looking forward to the day. She'd been looking forward to the weekend for at least a month. Her friend Meredith was coming over that morning to go pick apples and make applesauce with the Zook girls, and on Sunday, Sadie would be baptized. Counting her blessings as she dressed and headed downstairs to help with breakfast, Sadie hoped for a peaceful, fun, and beautiful weekend.

Greeting Miriam with a smile, Sadie decided that she had enough time to make fresh biscuits loaded with ham and cheese for a treat. As she stirred the flour, baking powder, milk, and shortening together, Sadie wondered what Meredith would think of spending the day with the Zooks. Meredith was such an unusual girl, and Sadie certainly hadn't planned on becoming good friends with a girl who was as far as you could get from Plain. Meredith was the oddest combination of curious and respectful that Sadie had ever encountered, and Sadie was looking forward to Meredith's meeting her family.

Sadie stirred in a little salt, a little sugar, and a handful each of cubed ham and shredded cheddar cheese. Adding in a little more milk to get just the right consistency, Sadie turned out the contents of the bowl onto the floured counter, rolled out the dough, and used a water glass to cut out perfect circles of biscuits that would bake up rich and buttery. She placed the biscuits on a baking sheet and moved them to the refrigerator until it was time for them to go in the oven.

Sadie checked on Miriam, who was slicing potatoes to go into the hot skillet on the stove and looked at the clock. "I'm going to collect baskets for apples. We'll need an extra for Meredith."

"I look forward to meeting Meredith. Is she ready for a full day's work?"

"Oh yes! I've explained to her that we'll spend at least a couple of hours picking, and then the real work begins when we get home. She promises that she is ready." Sadie left the kitchen, catching Hannah as she entered the room, tying on her apron. "Good morning, Mama."

Hannah smoothed out the folds in her apron. "Will Meredith be staying for dinner?"

"I believe so," Sadie answered. "I told her that she would be welcome. Even though she is not Plain, Mama, I think you will like her."

"I expect that I will," Hannah said with a smile.

Sadie gathered up baskets for apples and set them outside the kitchen door for use later. She woke Esther and helped the girl brush, braid, and pin up her hair while they discussed their plans for the day. Every year, the Zook girls would make the drive in their big open wagon to Brechnock Orchards, pick apples all morning, share a picnic, and return home to make applesauce. It was one of Sadie's favorite days of the year, and she was thrilled that Meredith wanted to join them.

When Esther was ready for the day, the girls headed downstairs to find breakfast nearly ready. Sadie slid her biscuits into the oven and sent Esther outside to ring the bell for the meal. After the men came inside, faces and hands scrubbed at the outdoor pump, Miriam put the golden brown biscuits on the table, and everyone sat down to eat.

Hannah looked at her husband, Samuel. "What do you and the boys have planned for today? Will you lay around in the shade all day since we will not be here to see you?"

"Hannah Zook! I am wounded. God would know, even if you didn't!" Samuel looked at his eldest son and namesake and added in a loud whisper, "But I'm not sure that your mother would be as merciful as the Lord."

Esther looked horrified at her father's blasphemy before she realized – based on the laughter from the rest of the family – that her father had been joking. She finally laughed as well, picturing her hard working father and brothers lazing about all day – a notion that was quite impossible. She looked at her mother. "Mama, can I drive the wagon today?" she asked.

"Maybe for a little part, Esther, but it is a long drive, and some of the roads are very busy. We must be extra careful."

Grinning at the prospect of piloting the wagon full of her sisters and mother, Esther resumed her breakfast and listened to the boys' plans to build a new shed for the gardening tools. As soon as everyone had finished eating, the men left the room to start their project. Esther helped her mother and sisters clear and clean up from breakfast. They also packed a picnic lunch and Sadie started watching out the window for Miriam's car. When the sleek, black Audi convertible entered the yard, Sadie dried her hands and went outside to greet Meredith.

"Okay to park here?" Meredith called out before she turned the car off.

"Yes. So glad you are here!" exclaimed Sadie.

"I stopped and picked up some doughnuts for breakfast," Meredith said as she hit the button to close the convertible's top. She got out of the car and asked Sadie, "Have you eaten?"

Sadie laughed. "Yes, we have. We've been up since 4:30 to get chores done. The doughnuts will be great in our picnic, though. That was thoughtful." Sadie noticed right away as Meredith got out of her car, that the English girl had carefully chosen her clothing for the day. Meredith wore jeans and a modestly cut long-sleeved t-shirt, rather than shorts and a strappy tank top. Sadie knew that the wardrobe was selected to ensure that none of Sadie's family would feel uncomfortable. Sadie took the box of doughnuts from Meredith. "Come meet my family!"

Introductions complete and doughnuts carefully packed into the picnic basket, the ladies headed outside to pile into the wagon. Isaac had hitched a pair of horses to their largest wagon, and since the day was sunny and warm, he had thoughtfully put up the canopy that covered most of the wagon's bed, providing shade and leaving the sides open for fresh air. Esther and Hannah climbed up front so that Esther could "help" drive, and Miriam, Sadie, and Meredith piled in the back with the empty apple baskets and their lunch.

Isaac looked with frank admiration at Meredith's Audi. "Are you sure you want to ride in this old wagon?" he asked the English girl. "Your car would be more comfortable," he said as if he couldn't imagine choosing to ride in anything other than the shiny sports car.

"No! I've been looking forward to this ever since Sadie invited me! This is so much fun!" Meredith answered with her customary enthusiasm. "To get to spend a day being Plain is such a treat!"

Miriam winked at Sadie before she turned to Meredith. "I have a dress and a bonnet you may borrow if you would like to look the part."

Meredith just giggled and politely declined the offer as Hannah allowed Esther to take the reins and urge the horses forward. The girls all waved to Isaac and the other men at the building site of the new shed as Esther skillfully eased the wagon out onto the road in front of the house.

Hannah took over the driving as they approached a busy crossroad, and Meredith noticed a small buggy approaching on the road they needed to cross. She wondered aloud if the Zooks knew the driver of the other buggy, and Sadie assured her that they most likely did. As the traffic was heavy on the road, their wagon was stuck at a red light, and before the light turned green, the buggy had reached them. Meredith watched Sadie's face fall as they realized that it was Abram Byler in the buggy.

"Good morning," Abram greeted them, stern-faced and solemn.

Hannah greeted the man politely, knowing that Sadie wouldn't wish to linger. After learning that Abram was headed into town to visit the hardware store, Hannah shared their plans for the day and prepared to move along. "We will see you at church tomorrow, Abram."

Abram waved and carefully avoided making eye contact with Sadie as he resumed his journey. Meredith and Miriam weren't sure if they should change the subject to make things easier for Sadie, or if she would want to discuss the meeting with Abram.

Sadie was aware of the girls closely watching her to see how she would react. "It is okay. I am fine. It has been months, and I am just fine," Sadie said as if she were convincing herself, rather than the other girls in the wagon. "Abram always looks so unhappy," Sadie noted softly. "I hope his mother is healthy."

Everyone knew, of course, that Ruth Byler had undergone surgery a few weeks before to remove the cancer that threatened her health. Meredith, being the daughter of a physician, was curious. "Has she started chemotherapy or radiation yet," she asked.

"I do not know. I don't really talk to Abram much. His parents don't approve, and he follows their direction still,"

Sadie answered, looking disappointed. "It is possible that we will hear more tomorrow at church."

"Well I hope she is seeing a good doctor. There are so many new specialists with new treatments, that Mom says she can hardly keep track of it all. She'd thought about oncology as a specialty, but she wanted to live in a small town and was afraid that she'd have to move us all to a big city if she specialized."

Sadie still marveled at the thought of having a mother who worked as much as Meredith's did, but her family seemed happy, and Sadie supposed that was what mattered. She didn't want that sort of life for herself and the children that she would have some day, but Meredith was proud of her mother and her little general practice in Ephrata.

"I hope she gets better, but let us talk of something else," Sadie suggested, trying to keep her thoughts of Abram from dampening her spirits. "Applesauce, spiced apples, pies…what else shall we make?"

Esther piped up from the front. "Mama, can we make apple pancakes for breakfast before church?"

The rest of the trip passed in discussion for the apples they would pick, and the girls' curious questions for Meredith. They discovered that her mother almost never cooked – a notion that mystified the girls. They were also surprised to discover that Meredith's father worked from home most days and he handled much of the laundry and cleaning.

Hannah ruefully thought to herself that a discussion with Esther needed to happen, perhaps Sunday afternoon, about the reasons why there were such clearly defined roles for Plain women and men, and the problems and complications that occurred in the English world as a result of shifting roles between genders. Meredith seemed like a nice girl, Hannah thought, but Esther was young and needed to have frequent reinforcement of the community's values to prevent the seven-year-old from looking with admiration at the outside world.

Esther crawled in the back of the wagon to play a game with the others and Hannah had a few moments to herself to think. She wondered how much Sadie had been bothered by seeing Abram. Hannah knew that it had to be difficult for Sadie to see Abram at practically every turn, given that he had abruptly ended their relationship a few months ago. She also thought about how blessed the family was that Sadie was a good and trustworthy girl. Sadie's role at Samuel's shop put her in contact with a steady stream of Englishers, and Sadie even had access to a telephone that she could have used for personal calls, had she chosen to.

Hannah knew, though, that Sadie had been raised with a strong sense of community and family, and with a warm loving environment that would help keep Sadie from looking outside their Plain community. Meredith was a harmless exception, Hannah hoped. She would just have to trust her daughter to refrain from bringing negative influences into their home.

When the horses and wagons finally pulled into the parking lot of the orchard, there were lots of minivans and SUVs full of families spending the day in the Pennsylvania countryside. The Brechnock Orchard was a favorite among Plain families, even though the owners were English, and Hannah drove the wagon over to an area where a few other horses and buggies had been parked. The girls got water for the horses, thirsty after their hour-and-a-half trek.

The girls each took a basket from the wagon's bed and headed toward the area where families were clustered waiting for the huge wagons to take them to the apple orchards. Meredith had never gone anywhere with a group of Amish girls, and she was extra aware of the attention that the Zooks received as they made their way to board the wagon. She noticed people staring, and she even noticed that a few people surreptitiously took pictures of the people in Plain dress.

Meredith leaned over to Sadie. "Does it ever bother you? The staring and the picture taking?"

Sadie smiled and shook her head. "Not really. If someone sticks a camera in my face, then yes, but it is normal for people to be curious about the way we live. We're different."

Meredith was surprised at Sadie's simple and honest response. She decided that if it didn't bother Sadie, then there was no reason why it should bother her. Meredith had wondered what it would be like to spend the entire day with Sadie's family. She had been meeting Sadie for lunch every couple of weeks and had enjoyed getting to know the Plain girl, but Meredith had not been sure that the rest of the girls would be as friendly and welcoming. Meredith felt lucky to get to share the girls' trip to the orchard and was even looking forward to the work of making a huge amount of applesauce that afternoon.

The girls all climbed up into the huge wagon that would transport them to the orchards. Though the wagon ride was nothing special for the Zooks, Meredith enjoyed the novelty of everything. Once the girls were settled, Hannah started giving instructions about which sorts of apples she wanted the girls to pick.

"We want McIntosh and Rome apples for applesauce, and I want Golden Delicious, Pink Lady, and Granny Smith for pies. If there are any Honey Crisp, let us get some of those as well. They may not be ripe yet, but we can take a look."

Apple game plan established, the girls climbed out of the wagons and found the orchard rows labeled with the apple varieties they wanted. Meredith partnered with Sadie, and she let the experienced girl lead the way. Sadie walked about halfway down the row of trees and stopped. Bees buzzed around the apples that head fallen and begun to decay on the ground, and Sadie looked around for a spare ladder.

"Here, hold my basket," Sadie called to Meredith as she moved to get a ladder. "I'll climb and hand apples down to you."

Content to catch the apples that Sadie picked and dropped in her direction, Meredith decided to test the waters and see if Sadie wanted to talk about Abram. "So do you and Abram not ever talk anymore?"

Sadie came down the ladder, repositioned it, and ascended again. "We talk. Just about work, though. I have tried to be friendly, but he just walks away or glares at me."

"Really? But you said he was kinda sweet?"

Sadie sighed. "He is, but he covers his sweetness up. It is buried deep down, and he will not let me see it again, since he has decided that our relationship was not part of God's plan."

"I still don't believe that he thinks that his mother's cancer was a sign from God. That's just crazy."

"It is hard for the English to understand sometimes, but we do believe that God has a plan for us, and we believe that we need to be open to seeing His plan. We do not always agree on what is truly a sign from God, though. That is the hard part."

"But can't you sit Abram down and set the man straight?"

Sadie stopped picking apples for a moment, and she rested her hands on the top of the ladder. "The short answer is no. If God's plan is for Abram and me to be together, then God will show Abram the truth. If that is not God's plan, then everything will work out the way it is supposed to."

"So you just leave it up to God?" Meredith asked skeptically.

"Exactly. God's will will be done if I just trust in Him and follow His commandments."

"So you don't have to worry? Everything just works out all on its own?"

"That is right," Sadie said with a smile, reaching to pull another ripe apple from the tree. "That does not mean it is always easy, but I know in my heart that if I trust in the Lord that everything will work out exactly as it is supposed to."

"Hm." Meredith grew quiet as she continued to catch the apples Sadie dropped to her. Meredith hadn't grown up religious – her mother was Jewish, and her father a lapsed Catholic, and religion had never been important enough to either of them to make a fuss over deciding how Meredith and her brother would be raised. Sadie's calm certainty showed Meredith why so many people sought out religion, though. That sense of peace that comes from knowing that there is a bigger plan, that God will take care of you – what a comfort! Meredith wasn't sure what – if anything – she believed, but she certainly found Sadie's faith intriguing.

Sadie came down from the ladder and checked to see how much space was in the baskets they'd brought. "We're nearly full. We can probably just do the rest from the ground." She took one of the baskets from Meredith, and started working her way around the tree, placing apples atop the others in the basket. "I hope that it is in God's plan that Abram and I might be together, but I will accept what happens."

Meredith picked apples from a branch near Sadie. "Don't you ever want to *make* something happen, though?"

Sadie smiled at Meredith. "I understand what you are asking, and it is just not our way. If God intends for Abram and me to be together it will happen."

The girls' baskets were finally full, and they looked

around for Hannah, Miriam, and Esther. They found Esther sitting at the end of a row of apple trees, two full baskets beside her. Hannah and Miriam joined them, sharing the weight of another full basket. The girls all loaded up their apples into the wagon, rode back, paid for the fruit based on the weight, and settled in the shade for a picnic lunch before their drive home.

❄ ❄ ❄

By day's end, Meredith wasn't sure she ever wanted to see another apple. She'd peeled, chopped, sliced, stirred, simmered, and baked apples in every way she could imagine. She felt proud that she had two jars of apple-sauce, sweetened with a little brown sugar and perfectly spiced with cinnamon, to take home with her. She also had a loaf of apple bread, and a jar of spiced apples with golden raisins. Her parents would be thrilled since they didn't often have home baked goodies.

Meredith didn't realize at first that she was visiting Sadie on an unusual day, because work wasn't divided up by gender in Meredith's home as it was in the Zooks'. Apple day was an exception, though, because it was the one day a year that the men cooked dinner while the women were inside taking up all the space in the kitchen with processing apples. The family sat down to dinner at the outside picnic tables and feasted on chicken, potatoes, and corn, all roasted in the outdoor wood-fired oven.

After Meredith helped clean up dinner, Isaac offered to help her carry her things to the car. Though Hannah worried that Isaac was a little too interested in Meredith's little sports car, she knew that Isaac would have to sort through the allure of material possessions for himself. Trusting Meredith to behave appropriately, Hannah nonetheless watched from the window.

Meredith thought about offering to take Isaac for a quick spin in the car he so obviously admired, but she thought that it might be more respectful to just thank the young man and go. "If you ever need a ride somewhere, just let me know," Meredith told Isaac as she slid into the driver's seat and lowered the top on the black convertible.

"Oh I will," Isaac replied. "I sure will."

Sadie and her sisters finished up their chores and prepared to bathe since they had church the next morning, and Sadie reflected on the day and the fun she'd had. Meredith had fit right in, even though she did ask a lot of questions. Sadie's smile faltered a bit when she thought back to the first time she'd met Meredith – that lovely June evening when Abram and Sadie had enjoyed such a carefree evening. It was that evening on which Sadie recalled, with a flush of heat, the stirrings of desire she had felt for Abram as she watched him stretched out on the picnic blanket. It was only a few days later that all of Sadie's tentative hopes of a future with Abram had been dashed by John and Ruth Byler's absolute prohibition of Abram and Sadie's relationship. With a sigh and a quick silent prayer for peace and patience, Sadie began unwinding her bun, unbraiding her hair, and preparing to wash the long, honey gold mass for church and her baptism in the morning.

Finally in bed with a head of still damp hair, Sadie

settled down to write a few lines in her journal. As tired as she was, she had a few thoughts that she wanted to capture.

Tomorrow I will be baptized and will become a full, adult member of the church. I am so pleased to know that I am making the decision to live Plain and humble for the rest of my life.

I am a little sad, though, because since I will be an adult, that means that I could be married if I wished. There is no man I wish to marry, though. I know that God would have me make the decision with my future in mind – a sober, hard working man who is humble and faithful to the Lord is all I need. Is it a sin to want more, though? Is it wrong to hope for a man with whom I can have interesting conversations about important things? Am I wrong to hope that I will feel some desire for the man who will be my husband and will be the father of my children?

I know that to focus on appearance is vain and foolish, but Abram Byler is a hard worker; he is devout; and he is tall and handsome and appealing to me. Is it too much to hope for another Abram to come along?

I want to pray that God will soften John and Ruth Byler's hearts, that He will show them that Abram and I would be a good match. But now I wonder if Abram even wants that anymore. He is so cold and distant that I do not even think that he would choose me if he could. It makes me sad, but I must trust that God will work everything out according to His plan.

I am glad that we had such a busy day today, so that I am tired enough to sleep even though I am excited about tomorrow.

Chapter Twenty-One

The family loaded up into two buggies, the Zooks set off for church on Sunday morning. Glad for another gorgeous early fall day, Sadie and her family sang hymns to pass the time as they drove for nearly forty-five minutes to arrive at the home of Jacob and Alice Sommer, a new family in their church. This Sunday was the first time that they would worship in the Sommer's home, and everyone was a little curious to see what their home would look like. Since Alice hadn't been raised in the Amish faith, Sadie wondered if there would be traces of her worldly past in their house.

Typically this week's meeting would have been in the home of Elijah and Emma Lapp, but as Emma was expecting the couple's second child any day, the Sommers had volunteered to open their home instead. Jacob had grown up in nearby Lancaster, but Alice was originally from Portland, Oregon. Sadie and Miriam were curious about how the couple had met, and they looked forward to getting to know Alice better. They hadn't had any outsiders move to their community recently, so the urge to get to know them and their four children was strong.

Young Samuel had arrived just a few minutes before the rest of the family, and he was waiting to help his father with the horse. The two Sommer boys, Stephen, aged twenty and Seth, aged sixteen, helped handle the horses as people arrived for the service. The girls carried in the food for the communal meal that would follow the service and the baptisms, greeting Alice and her daughter, Stella, aged eighteen, in the kitchen.

Sadie went into the living room, where the benches for the church service were set up. She made her way over to the four other young people who would be baptized that day. They'd been preparing for weeks, studying the foundations of their religion and the *ordnung*, the communal rules they were committing to live by. Each one of them had been looking forward to this day for quite some time. Sadie watched the rest of the congregation enter, thinking to herself that at the next church service, she would be with the other adult women, greeting each of her sisters with a holy kiss.

Sadie watched carefully as Ruth and Sarah Byler arrived, noticing that Ruth looked tired and drawn. Sarah waved to Sadie, but Ruth's eyes passed over Sadie as if she were invisible. With a little sigh, Sadie sat down next to the others awaiting baptism and thought to herself that Ruth would probably never like her. Resolving to cease worrying about it and turn the problem over to God, Sadie folded her hands and thought about the ritual she was about to go through. Unable to help herself, Sadie turned to watch for Abram to enter the room, and he sat down next to his father without even a glance in Sadie's direction. Both Abram and John looked tired and preoccupied, and Sadie wondered if perhaps things weren't going well for Ruth.

The service started, and the congregation joined together in song. After the first two sermons, the five young people who were to be baptized came forward and knelt in front of the Bishop and his wife. As Sadie and the others vowed to uphold the *ordnung* and forsake the world, she felt as though she was becoming part of something much larger than herself, larger than her family, even. As the Bishop anointed each of their heads with water, and as the girls rose to receive a holy kiss from the Bishop's wife, and the boys to receive a kiss from the Bishop, himself, Sadie felt joyous and at peace.

Through the last brief sermon and the last of the hymns, Sadie felt suffused with love and warmth. She was fully a Sister to all of the members of their congregation. Sadie was surprised at the end of the service when John Byler stood and walked to the front of the room.

He was blunt. "You all know that Ruth has been sick and has had surgery. The doctor has told us that he probably removed all of the cancer, but there are a number of treatment options that are available, some of which involve some specialists with new methods. Our family has decisions to make – about whether to try to find one of these specialists, or whether to go with more traditional methods that may or may not be effective. We ask for your prayers for the Lord to guide us in making these difficult decisions."

John Byler said his piece and walked through the room and out the door. He was clearly troubled and trying to contain his emotions. Sadie sat still, stunned by the news that Ruth's condition might require special treatment. Sadie ached for Abram, and she could clearly imagine how worried she would be if it were Hannah who were sick.

As the congregation filtered out of the room, men to the outdoors to await their lunch, and women to the kitchen to get the food ready, Sadie looked for Abram. She saw him, still at the edge of the living room, talking to Luke Stoltzfos and looking uncomfortably stiff. Sadie wondered for a split second if she should approach him, and she immediately realized that concern for one of her Brothers was a pure and acceptable reason for initiating a conversation. Abram watched Sadie approach him from across the room. He couldn't decide whether to greet her or flee from the room. As Luke was in the middle of a sentence, Abram felt stuck and could only watch, helpless as Sadie walked his way.

Sadie waited until Luke had finished speaking. "Abram, I am so sorry to hear of your mother's continued sickness. Did the doctor give you an idea of how likely it is that she will recover completely?"

Abram stood up straighter, though he was already taller than everyone else in the room. "Thank you Sadie. He thinks they removed all of the cancer with the surgery, but this kind of cancer is almost certain to return if she does not receive further treatment. He knows that there are some aggressive new methods that might work better, but that may require seeing a specialist in a big city."

Luke spoke up. "Well if it is a matter of transportation, or of finances, you know that you can count on your Brothers and Sisters."

"Thank you, Luke. It is more a matter of Mother deciding how much treatment she is willing to suffer through. Most of the treatments – chemotherapy and radiation, both – will make her feel sick and tired, and she must decide for herself how much she is willing to endure."

Sadie had to restrain her impulse to put her hand on Abram's arm. "But if it makes her better in the end, then surely it is worth it?"

Abram looked down at Sadie, realizing how much he had missed her blue eyes and freckled nose. "The doctor seems to think that some of these new treatments will work better on the cancer and be easier on her body. God alone knows, though. We must pray for guidance."

"Abram, you and your family will have my prayers."

Sadie was surprised to hear a woman's voice right behind her, and as Sadie turned, she was even more surprised to see that it was Ruth Byler who addressed her.

"Sadie, we thank you. We will take all the prayers we can get. Abram, your father is looking for you." Ruth Byler turned and walked away without saying another word. Sadie looked at Abram, wide-eyed at Ruth's surprisingly civil remark.

Abram looked back, sinking a little deeper than necessary into Sadie's gaze. "Thank you Sadie. I am sure that God will show us the way. I cannot help but wish that we knew someone…that there were one of these specialists here in Ephrata, as Mother is less likely to want to seek treatment in a big city."

Lacing her fingers together to keep from reaching for Abram, Sadie replied softly. "If it is God's will, He will find a way, Abram."

As Abram turned to go find his father, Sadie realized that despite her elation at her baptism, her feelings were a swirling mess. She had so missed talking to Abram, but she was so saddened by the topic of Ruth's cancer. Sadie felt all mixed up and decided that she needed to calm herself before lunch was served.

Sadie glanced around the room and decided that she could manage to sneak out without being questioned. There were plenty of women, talking, laughing, and ensuring that lunch would get on the tables. Since most of the traffic was in and around the kitchen and the kitchen door to the yard, Sadie slipped to the front door that opened on the opposite side of the house. She stepped outside and was relieved to see no one except a few children playing in the far corner of the yard.

Sadie sat down on the steps and rested her elbows on her knees and her chin on her hands. Would she never get over Abram? Would every single conversation she had with him for the rest of her life be fraught with the electricity that seemed to connect the two of them? Sadie realized that as much as she wanted to be patient and trust in the Lord, that the only real chance she had of moving on from her attraction to Abram was in finding another young man to capture her attention. Lost in her thoughts, Sadie was startled when the door behind her opened.

Sadie turned to see Stephen Sommer step outside and take a seat next to her on the steps. She had never really spoken with Stephen before, though they had been introduced a few months before when the Sommers had moved to Ephrata.

"Congratulations on your baptism, Sadie. I remember the day I was baptized."

"Thank you, Stephen. It is wonderful to be a full member of the community."

"I hope that I am not being too forward, but you look a little sad for a girl who was just baptized," Stephen observed aloud.

Sadie was surprised at such a personal observation from someone she didn't know particularly well.

Stephen watched her and gauged her reaction accurately. "I apologize. I can see that you do not want to discuss whatever is on your mind."

"You do not need to apologize. It is just that I am unused to people being so direct," Sadie answered with a little smile.

Just as Sadie smiled at Stephen, and just before she could speak again, Abram rounded the corner of the house, as if he were on a mission. He saw Sadie and Stephen on the steps, saw Sadie's smile, and Abram stopped dead in his tracks. He instantly looked deflated, as if someone had just delivered crushing news to him.

Sadie watched as he looked at her, crestfallen, and turned to shuffle back around the house.

Hand to her mouth, Sadie looked as if she was ready to jump up and run after Abram just as the dinner bell rang. Figuring that she would find a way to talk to Abram before the day's end, Sadie turned and ran inside, leaving a puzzled Stephen sitting alone on the steps. Sadie scanned the rooms as she entered, looking for Abram inside. As she got to the kitchen, she saw that tables were set outdoors as well, but before she could look for Abram outside, she was hailed by Miriam and felt compelled to sit next to her sister.

Sadie held polite conversation with the people at her table, but her thoughts were occupied by Abram. He had looked so disappointed when he'd rounded the corner and had seen her in conversation with Stephen. Sadie wanted to explain to him that there was nothing between her and the new young man. She did feel a little indignant, though, that Abram would expect her not to have private conversations with other men. Abram was, after all, the one who had rejected Sadie, rather than the other way around.

If Sadie were a crueler sort of girl, she knew that she could make a show and give Abram a reason to be jealous, but Sadie wasn't built that way. She wouldn't deliberately hurt Abram, and in fact she couldn't wait to find him and let him know that she and Stephen weren't an item. Lost in her thoughts, Sadie realized that everyone at the table was looking at her, as if they expected her to say something.

"I am sorry, what?"

Alice Sommer laughed. "I was just saying that now that you're baptized, we'll expect you to get married and start a family. Do you have a husband on the horizon?"

Sadie blushed prettily and shook her head. "No, no husband-to-be, I am afraid. Maybe I will be an old maid and Auntie Sadie to all the children."

Alice looked a little surprised. "Hmm. Maybe we will have to find a young man for you, then."

Miriam sensed that Sadie needed to be rescued and deftly shifted the conversation to another topic. "Speaking of young men, has Stella settled on anyone?"

Alice laughed again. "Not just yet, though she is happy to be here. She hadn't found anyone to her liking where we lived in Lancaster before we moved here. I think she has her eye on several boys."

As soon as the meal was over, Sadie was quick to leave the table. As she helped clear dishes, she kept an eye out for Abram. Hoping she'd be able to catch him for a chat before he and his family left, Sadie worked quickly and scooted out of the kitchen at her first opportunity. She was very disappointed when she finally escaped only to see the back of Abram's little courting buggy as it pulled out of the Sommers' yard and onto the road. He drove away without a backward glance, and Sadie was sorry to have missed her chance to talk to him and set things straight.

The rest of the day passed much as a typical Sunday did. Sadie was pleased to return home and have some free time to spend with a book out on the porch swing, soaking up the September sun and enjoying some peace and quiet. As she reflected on her day – the wonderful, inclusive feeling of having been baptized and the frantic need she'd felt to set things straight between Abram and herself, Sadie realized that the only thing she could do was turn her problems over to the Lord and know that if she had enough faith, that things would work out according to His will. Sadie said a quick prayer of thanksgiving for the peace that she felt in giving her problems to God, and she returned to reading her book.

Chapter Twenty-Two

When Sadie and Samuel arrived at Ephrata Woodworks on Monday morning, Sadie could tell right away that Abram was troubled. He unhitched their horse from their buggy, and he fed and watered the horse, all without making eye contact with Sadie. Though Abram was never socially adept, he seemed even more awkward than usual. As Sadie lifted the lunch basket form the buggy, she saw that Samuel had already gone inside the workshop, and Sadie seized her opportunity, and set the basket down.

"Abram, can I talk with you for a moment?"

"I am very busy. I left in the middle of a project."

"Abram." Sadie waited, silent, until he finally looked at her. "It will just take a minute, but I really want to talk to you."

"Fine," the young man replied abruptly. "What is it?"

"First of all, how is your mother?"

Abram signed and shook his head. "She is stubborn and set in her ways. She has decided that she will only seek out treatment that she can get locally. She won't hear of traveling to find a specialist who might do her more good."

"Oh, I am so sorry to hear that," Sadie said softly. She longed to touch Abram, and make the connection that they both still felt even stronger, but she had resolved, even promised, that she wouldn't make the separation more difficult for Abram.

"It is frustrating, but it must be God's will."

"But don't you think that sometimes God wants you to make an effort to help yourself, that it might be His will to go seek out the help you need?"

Abram looked at Sadie as if were the first time he'd ever laid eyes on her. "Sadie, you do have a different way of looking at things. I do not think my parents see it that way."

"Well, you will let me know if there is anything I can do to help, right?"

"Sure," Abram answered, and the tone of his voice made it clear that he didn't think that Sadie would have any help to offer him or Ruth.

"The other thing is, I saw the look on your face when you came around the corner at the Sommers' house yesterday. When I was talking to Stephen."

"I have no claim on you, Sadie. You can talk to anyone you like."

"I know, Abram, but I want you to know that there is nothing between me and Stephen. Nothing like there is between you and me."

Abram laughed, his face telling the truth – that he

found no humor in this conversation. "Like there *was* between us. Was, not is."

Sadie looked at the ground before meeting Abram's eyes again. "Was. You are right. In any case, there is nothing between me and Stephen."

"Fine, Sadie. That is your business, not mine."

Sadie's irritation with Abram – his timidity, his acceptance of what he perceived as his lot in life – threatened to boil over. "Abram, have you ever stopped to think that maybe you are wrong? That maybe you have misread the signs that God has sent you?"

Abram's mouth fell open as he gaped at Sadie and her bold words

"Did you ever stop to think that maybe God has given you a challenge to overcome, rather than a sign that you should sit back and passively accept whatever happens? Did you ever think that maybe you have a chance to use the opportunities that God has given you to be happy?"

Abram looked at Sadie and was utterly confused, just full of questions. What if she was right? What if he had read the signs all wrong?

Sadie was on a roll, all of the words she'd suppressed for months spilling out all at once. "Abram, maybe you should start looking for signs that God wants you to be happy? What if it was a sign that you found my journal? Did you ever think of that?"

Abram could hardly figure out what to say, but he knew that he should stop Sadie before her raised voice turned to a full-fledged shout and brought her father back outside. Abram leaned in and placed his hands on

Sadie's shoulders, the heat of his touch the only force that he knew could stop the torrent of words. "Sadie, stop."

Sadie fell silent, and she felt like a magnet held the two of them together. She was surprised by Abram's touch, and by the way it made her feel. She was aware of the weight and heat from his hands, and her face started to flush as she realized just how close they were standing.

Uncomfortable with the heat and intensity of Sadie's gaze, Abram reluctantly removed his hands from her shoulders and took a step back. "You have, once again, given me a lot to think about."

Sadie realized that she had gone too far and had crossed a line with Abram. "I am sorry. I lost my temper, and I am sorry, Abram. I had no right to say what I did."

"I think you had every right, Sadie, and I will think on what you have said, and I will pray to God for guidance. Maybe He will give me a sign that you are right."

Sadie didn't know what else she should, or could, say, so she simply slipped her arm through the handle of the lunch basket and headed for the store. Abram watched her go, and it was if all of the discipline he'd exercised for the last few months had evaporated. He'd been so careful to limit his contact with Sadie to the absolute minimum, and he'd focused on losing himself in hard work and prayer for his mother, but one touch, and he'd come undone.

Abram followed the young woman with his eyes, watching as she balanced the basket on her hip while she fumbled with her key. He felt warm – much warmer than he should on a September morning. Abram was horrified to discover that he couldn't help but devour Sadie with his gaze. He knew that focusing on her body wasn't appropriate, but he simply couldn't help but notice the curve of her hip and the graceful line of her neck. Abram shook his head, engaged his self control, and told himself to get back to work.

Flustered and frustrated, Sadie finally managed to get her key in the door, and she was relieved to disappear inside her store. For the most part, what happened in the store made sense, could be neatly organized, and went according to plan. Given the swirl of emotions that Sadie was trying to leave outside the door, she relished a little order and control.

Unless there was a critical task that required her attention, Sadie always began her workday the same way. She stowed the lunch basket, readied her paper and pen, and hit the button to play the messages that had accumulated on the answering machine over the weekend.

"Um...good morning. Um...I'm sorry, I didn't expect an answering machine at an Amish store. Anyway, my wife is expecting our first child, and I want to get her a rocking chair. If you could call me back and let me know if you do rocking chairs, that would be great. Thanks."

Sadie jotted down the name and phone number and smiled to herself. It always amused Sadie that customers were so surprised that an Amish business would have a phone and even an air conditioner in the store for the comfort of shoppers. She hit the button for the next message.

"*Hi, Sadie, it's Jack Foster. I don't know if you remember me, but I have a table and chairs on order from you. They're supposed to be delivered sometime in the next couple of weeks, but I'm going to be in Ephrata this Wednesday, and I thought that if they're ready, I could just pick them up. If you'd call me back and let me know, I'd surely appreciate it.*"

Sadie waited, pen in hand for Jack to leave his phone number, but the machine beeped to indicate the end of the message. Scrunching up her nose, Sadie put a star next to the message as a reminder to herself that she would need to look up the sales ticket for the contact information, and she moved on to the next message. By the time she was finished taking notes from the machine, she'd filled most of the page. Business had been very good of late, and Samuel and Sadie had discussed raising their rates to perhaps slow down the volume of work. As it was, they had customers on a waitlist for custom pieces. Sadie marveled that they now required a minimum of a month wait for custom pieces, with larger projects requiring six months to complete. The shop was just too busy to push their handcrafted furniture through any quicker. Sadie thought that she remembered the order for Jack Foster, so she started flipping through the tickets from June.

She pulled out the paperwork on the dining table and ten chairs for Jack, and looked at his business card that she'd stapled to the ticket rather than copying all of his information. "Dr. Jack Foster, M.D.," she read from the first line. The second line read, "Oncologist." The third: "Fox Chase Cancer Center, Philadelphia, PA."

Sadie let the ticket fall to the counter. What were the odds, she wondered of her father's little woodworking shop having a client who specialized in oncology? She knew that Ruth had decided not to seek medical care from out of town, but Sadie wondered if somehow, some way, this little connection might not be a sign from God. What if Ruth did need more help than she could get in little Ephrata? Maybe Jack Foster was the key.

Not sure if she was ridiculous for being a little excited, Sadie ran out the door and across the yard to the workshop. She didn't want to get Abram's hopes up, and she didn't want to explain the whole situation, which, if she thought about it, seemed a little tenuous and silly, but she felt like she was being moved to explore this option.

"Da," Sadie shouted as she entered, not realizing how loud she'd sound in the quiet shop with only hand tools in use. Lowering her voice, she continued. "Da, when will the Foster table and chairs be done? He's going to be in town this week and if they'll be ready, he can pick them up instead of having them shipped to Philadelphia."

Samuel put down the hammer and chisel he'd been using and went to the calendar he kept hanging over his workbench. He took it down, ran his index finger over a few of the entries, and answered Sadie. "Hm. It is all assembled and just needs to be finished. If I put Abram on it, we can have it ready by Wednesday."

"Oh, he will be thrilled. He'll be here to pick it up

on Wednesday, then. Thanks, Da." Feeling suffused with hope, Sadie winked at Abram as she left, savoring the look of surprise on the man's face as she closed the door. When Sadie got back inside the store, she stood behind the counter for a few moments, hand on the telephone.

She realized that her response to her customer's profession was an emotional one, and Sadie felt compelled to calm herself down. She ran through what she knew for sure. She knew that Ruth was sick. She knew that Ruth had forced Abram to stop seeing Sadie, and that Ruth would probably not welcome Sadie's interference in private matters. Sadie knew that there were cancer treatments out there that might be Ruth's best chance at survival. She knew that God could do wonderful things with the lives of the people who trust and believe in Him.

Sadie held her breath for a moment, barely able to believe what she was thinking. Could it be God's will that had put all of these things together? Could God want her to act? Could God be working to heal Ruth and to perhaps even smooth the way for Abram and Sadie to be together? Maybe God was telling Sadie that everything would work out as He planned if only she did her little part. Sadie decided that she would forge ahead, look for signals and signs from God, and above all, have faith.

She picked up the phone and dialed the number for Jack Foster. She'd already decided that the conversation would be purely professional and that her only role should be in setting things in motion. She needed to get

Jack into the store, and she needed to get Abram in the same room. When Sadie hung up the phone, she was pleased with her decision. She had gotten things in place, and God would take care of the rest.

❀ ❀ ❀

For two days it had felt to Sadie like Wednesday was never going to arrive. She had decided not to tell Abram about the significance of Jack's visit to the store and the outcome for which she so fervently hoped. Sadie was beside herself all morning, hardly able to concentrate, and pleased that she had nothing too taxing to work on. Lunch seemed to drag out forever, and while Abram and Samuel both noticed that Sadie was distracted, neither man enquired as to why.

When Sadie finally saw the big van pull into the parking lot, she took a deep breath and resolved to handle her customer's business first before she brought Abram in and brought up the subject of Ruth. Jack opened the door, and Sadie was surprised to realize that she hadn't remembered that Jack had been the topic of one of her journal entries months before. Deciding that the fact that Jack was gay shouldn't have any bearing on the business they had to discuss, Sadie put it out of her mind.

Jack Foster opened the door to the store and poked his head inside. "Hey, Sadie. Should I park here or over by the shop?" he called out.

"There is fine. I had Abram bring your table and chairs into the store, and he'll help you load them into your van. Come on in!"

Jack walked inside and closed the door behind him. "It's good to see you again. Thanks for rushing the table. It wasn't an emergency, but I figured that since I was going to be in town, I'd save us the trouble and expense of shipping."

Sadie looked at Jack and knew for sure that she had done the right thing in planning to get him and Abram together. Jack was warm, open, and friendly, and Sadie just knew that God had put him in their shop for a reason. "I am glad we could shift things around and finish your table earlier. Have a seat, and we'll finish up the paperwork and final payment, and then I will go fetch Abram to help you."

Jack sat down at the table Sadie had directed him to, and he sighed as he settled down. "I guess I could have gotten the table next week or the week after. I didn't know it at the time, but there was no reason to rush it."

Sadie was puzzled. "Really? You will be in town next week too?"

"Yeah. Not for fun, though. I'm an oncologist – a doctor who treats cancer – and my sister is sick. She is home with two little ones, and she can't travel to Philly every week for her treatments. She's my sister and my best friend, so I agreed to come down and treat her here, at her doctor's office."

Sadie sat down heavily, absolutely stunned. She opened her mouth but no sound emerged.

Jack looked at her, waited a few seconds and finally spoke. "Sadie. You okay?"

She managed to close her mouth, cover it it with her

hands in disbelief, and she looked at Jack, blue eyes wide as could be. "I can hardly believe it."

"What? What's wrong?"

"You won't believe this, but I was so excited that you were coming in because there is someone I want you to meet." Sadie stood up, deciding that she would rather explain herself just once. "I will be right back." She dashed out of the room, and Jack stayed at the table, curious and confused.

When Sadie opened the door again, she brought Abram with her. Jack stood as she introduced the two men.

Abram thought he was there simply as muscle, so he looked at Jack. "Ready to get loaded up?"

Sadie interrupted Abram. "Wait. Abram, you will not believe what the Lord has done for you and your family. Jack is a doctor. An oncologist."

Abram appraised Jack and was silent for a few moments before he finally spoke. "It is nice to meet you. My mother has cancer. Had cancer. Well, she has had surgery and we are trying to decide what treatments would be best for her." Abram turned to Sadie. "I do not know why you thought I needed to meet another doctor."

"But Abram, he is a specialist, and he is in town one day a week to treat his sister. You said that Ruth wouldn't leave town to find a specialist, but what if the specialist came to her?" The words left Sadie all in a rush, and she stood still, a bit amazed at her audacity in having brought the topic up so suddenly.

Jack held up a hand, as if he wanted to stop Sadie from saying another word. "Sadie, wait a minute. Oncology is very specialized, and I might not even be the right person to treat Abram's mother."

"You are." Sadie was as calm as she could be. "I know you are."

Abram looked at Sadie, thunder in his gaze. "Sadie, can I talk to you outside?"

Outside in the parking lot, Abram turned, angry at Sadie's interference, only to see Sadie's clear confident blue eyes and a hopeful smile on her face.

"Sadie, did you ever stop to think that maybe my mother would not want you meddling in her affairs?"

Sadie answered simply. "Yes."

"But you did it anyway? Why would you call this man out of nowhere and bring him here to treat my mother?"

"But Abram, I didn't bring him here. God did. All I did was put the two of you together. It is God's plan, not mine."

Abram was clearly frustrated, and he shook his head. "Sadie, what on earth are you talking about?"

"Do you remember the talk we had on Monday? About trusting that God would work everything out according to His plans?"

"Of course."

"Right after we spoke, I went in and checked the answering machine. Jack had left a message and wanted to pick up his table early. It was when I looked for his number to return the call that I noticed his profession on his business card."

"So he is a doctor. Sadie, He happens to treat cancer. That is not unusual, and that does not mean that God wants this doctor to treat my mother."

"But that's not all, Abram. He is an oncologist, and he has made arrangements to come treat his sister every single week. All the way from Philadelphia! Abram, clearly God has made these things happen so that your mother can get the treatment she needs without having to leave Ephrata. Don't you see?"

Abram just stared at Sadie, unable to come up with a single thing to say. Could she be right? Was it possible that Sadie had found an answer to his family's prayers? That God had worked through her to find a way to save Ruth's life? If that were true, then what did that mean for Abram and Sadie? Could it be that Abram had been completely wrong? He hardly dared to hope it.

"I do not know what to say," Abram said, realizing that Sadie was expecting him to say something.

"What do you think?"

"I do not know what to think. I think that I hope you are right, but I am afraid to get too excited over this idea before I know if it could possibly work."

Sadie looked at Abram and boldly put her hand on his forearm. "Will you promise me that you will think about it? Maybe we can just ask Jack if he will agree to meet with your mother."

Abram looked at Sadie's hand on his arm, and he felt all at once like the temperature outside had risen twenty degrees and he was having trouble breathing. "I will think about it. Of course I will think about it." Abram felt electrified, strangely full of energy and suffused with hope. "Sadie, I hope that you are right. I hope that God put Jack in that store for a reason." He covered her hand with his, pressing the back of her hand with his palm. "And I hope that you are right about God wanting us to be happy."

Sadie beamed at Abram, grabbed his hand, and pulled him back inside the store to talk to Jack.

Chapter Twenty-Three

Abram sat on the edge of his bed, trying to think through the best approach to bringing up the idea of meeting with Dr. Foster. Jack had been surprisingly easy to convince that meeting with Ruth was a good idea. Abram laughed out loud as he thought that you'd have to be a fool to stand in Sadie's way when she had God on her side. Jack had agreed to meet with Ruth and John and review her case. Jack had also promised that if the Bylers were amenable, that Jack would meet with Ruth's doctor and discuss treatment possibilities. Abram couldn't have asked for any more, but he knew his biggest challenge would be in convincing his parents to consider his plan.

Realizing that the best approach was just to jump in with both feet, Abram stood, squared his shoulders and decided to try to get his parents together to talk before breakfast. Abram was concerned about Ruth, and not just because he was worried about ensuring that her cancer didn't return. Ruth hadn't seemed like herself of late. She'd never been cheerful or joyous, but lately she had withdrawn even more than usual. She had seemed down and unhappy.

If his family were more like Sadie's, Abram thought that he might have been able to ask his mother what was wrong, but the Bylers weren't particularly open. They led disciplined lives, all working together for the good of the entire family, but there was very little of the easy companionship that Abram felt at the Zook's home. Abram had actually been surprised to discover that he enjoyed the playful affection of the Zook's interactions, and he wondered if he could do anything to soften his parents' hearts.

Abram walked into the kitchen, where Ruth and Sarah were getting breakfast started. "Mother, can you spare a few minutes? I'd like to talk to you and Father."

"Of course. Sarah can handle breakfast. If you will go get your father, I'll get these biscuits in the oven."

Abram nodded at his mother and headed outside to the barn to find John. He wasn't exactly looking forward to the discussion he needed to have, but after the talk he'd had with Sadie the day before, Abram felt revitalized, stronger. He felt as though he'd been given a gift of insight that he'd never been privy to before. Sadie had opened his eyes to the possibility that if he had faith and trusted in God, that God's plan for his life might just be a wonderful one.

Abram and his father came inside and went into the parlor to sit and talk. Deciding that nothing would be gained by waiting around, Abram just dove in.

"Mother, I know that you have made your decision, and that you have decided not to look for treatment out of town. I understand why you made that decision, and I respect it. But something happened yesterday that may change everything. I have to ask you to open your heart and mind to the Lord and listen to what I have to tell you."

John and Ruth looked at one another. Abram almost seemed like a different person. He spoke with confidence and conviction, and his parents were compelled to listen to him.

"I met a doctor yesterday at the shop – an oncologist. He lives in Philadelphia, but he was picking up some furniture he had ordered from us. He was in town, and will be in town once a week, to treat his sister who lives here. From what I understand, he works at one of the best cancer facilities in the world, and the fact that he is here, and that he is willing to meet with you and your doctor… well, that can only be the Hand of God at work."

John looked at his wife. "Wait a minute, son. You mean that you talked to him about your mother? And that he agreed to see her?"

"Yes! He warned us that he might not be able to do anything for you, Mother, but he did agree to the meeting."

Ruth narrowed her eyes. "Us?" she asked.

Abram knew that Sadie's involvement in the meeting with Jack might be a problem for Ruth, but he was determined to stand up for what he believed to be right. "Us. Mother, Sadie is the one who discovered that our customer is a doctor. She knew that he would be stopping in the store, and she introduced us. She was certain, and I agree with her, that we are seeing God working in our lives."

Ruth looked at her son. She looked at John. She opened her mouth as if to speak, but she didn't say a word. She stood, crossed the room, and just before she reached the doorway, she turned to her husband and son. "I need a few moments to myself."

John looked at Abram, surprised by Ruth's reaction. "So it was Sadie who put this in motion?"

"Yes, Father. It was. I know that you and Mother think that Sadie is worldly and proud, but you do not understand her. She is earnest and has great faith that God works in our lives. She believes that this is one of those instances, and I have to say that I agree. I was skeptical at first, but I prayed about it last night, and I believe that Dr. Foster is here because God wants Mother to live."

"Putting the issue of Sadie aside, I cannot see how this Dr. Foster can be anything but a blessing. I will not force Ruth to go see him, but I hope she will want to."

Abram sighed in relief. "I am so glad you see it that way. I was worried that you would not want to hear about it since it was Sadie who worked it out."

"I have learned, though I sometimes need a reminder, that I should pay the most attention to my own behavior and worry less about the behavior of others – with certain limits of course. That does not mean that I would tolerate terrible acts by a member of the congregation."

"Oh, Father," Abram said with irritation. "I do not need a lecture. I wonder what is keeping Mother."

"She has tried to hide her troubles from you and your siblings, but this cancer has been very hard on her. She has told me that she has spent a lot of time in prayer, asking God what she did to deserve to be so sick."

"But she can't possibly believe..." Abram trailed off, rather than finishing the sentence.

"I do not know, son. You know your mother. She doesn't engage in idle talk, and that means that sometimes I have no idea what she is thinking."

"Well I guess I will go get some chores done before breakfast, then. I hope I can talk to Mother before I leave for work, but I guess I should not disturb her."

As Abram stood and put his straw hat on, John looked at his son. He rarely praised his children, wanting to keep them from growing too proud, but he felt as though he should make an exception this morning. "You have grown up into a fine young man, Abram."

Surprised at his father's uncharacteristic praise, Abram nodded to acknowledge the comment, and he left the room to get to work. Abram and his brothers did the very same chores that they did every morning, and by the time they heard the breakfast bell ring, they were hungry and needed to wash up. Though Abram could tell that his brothers were curious about his conversation with their parents, he chose not to discuss it with them. He didn't want to get their hopes up about Ruth's treatment, especially when he didn't know how his mother would react to the news he'd given her.

As Abram dried his hands, he wondered if Ruth would be at breakfast. He sat down at the table, and ate with his family, but Ruth's chair remained empty. In fact, it wasn't until breakfast was over and cleaned up that Ruth reappeared downstairs. She approached Abram and spoke softly, words intended for his ears alone.

"I have thought it over, and I will go see your Doctor Foster. I have other matters on my mind as well, and I have some praying to do today. I will want to speak with you when you return home from work."

Abram nodded at his mother and departed for work. As his buggy followed the horse along the winding, rural roads to town, Abram mulled over his situation. Sadie's words had opened his eyes in a way, and he wanted to be more open to the different things that the Lord might be telling him. He was fixated on the idea that it might actually be God's will that he and Sadie get together, but he found himself perplexed. How was he supposed to tell the difference between his own desires, that might be selfish and counter to God's plans, and God's will for him?

He knew that feelings were unreliable, unstable, and self-indulgent. Sadie seemed to think that you could use your feelings as an indicator, though – that her feelings for Abram might be confirming what God intended. Abram had never considered such a notion, and he felt as though he were treading water, miles from shore, with no land in sight. He wasn't sure what direction to go, and he was having trouble figuring out what he should do. In fact, the only two things that Abram could be sure of was that he wanted his mother to get better, and that he wanted to be with Sadie.

Abram was hard at work when he heard the Zook's buggy pull into the yard. He hurried outside to help with the horse, and he could tell that Sadie was anxious to talk to him. He took care of the horse and followed Sadie into the store.

Sadie couldn't wait to find out if Abram had talked to his parents. "So? Did you talk to them?"

"I did. "

"And?"

Abram discovered that he enjoyed Sadie's curiosity. It felt good to have her hanging on his words, excited to learn what he knew. "Mother agreed to see Dr. Foster."

Sadie was surprised. She'd expected that Abram would come in to work and report that he'd been unable to convince his mother to see Jack. "Really? Wow, that is wonderful."

"Yes. I was surprised. Mother is acting a little strangely though. She said she wants to talk to me this evening, and I have no idea what it's about."

"Well what is important is that she will see Jack. It is a good thing that she doesn't know that I suggested it, or she would have refused for sure."

"Sadie, that is part of her strange behavior. She does know. I told her."

Sadie looked puzzled. "She knows that I was involved, and she wasn't angry?"

"No, she did not seem angry. We didn't talk very long, but she seemed like she really had a lot on her mind. I am just so relieved that she will see Dr. Foster. I feel like a weight has been lifted from my shoulders, and I am so thankful that you have set all of this in motion."

Sadie shook her head. "It is not my doing. It is the work of the Lord."

Abram couldn't help himself, and he took two steps to close the space between Sadie and him. Feeling bold and more certain than he usually did, Abram reached down and took Sadie's hand. "You have the open heart and mind that is needed to realize when God is working through you, Sadie. You are very special, and you are very special to me."

Enjoying the feel of her hand in Abram's, Sadie looked up at him and smiled. "I am pleased to hear you say that, Abram. I have missed you, and I hope that if the Lord is willing we can share some more conversations."

Abram squeezed her hand and returned her smile. "I think that may be possible, and I am glad. I expect that I will know more about my parents' position on things this evening after I talk to Mother."

Reluctantly letting go of Sadie's hand, Abram turned and walked toward the door. "I should let you get to work, and Samuel will be expecting me."

"I will see you at lunch, Abram."

"I am looking forward to it."

Sadie started her workday with a smile, making a list of the tasks she wanted to accomplish by day's end. She was pleased to note that she would probably have time to sit down for a few minutes and write in her journal. She always felt like writing about what was going on in her life helped her see things more clearly, and she certainly could use a little clarity.

Ready to tackle the first item on her list, Sadie was startled when the door flew open. Her father rushed inside, and Sadie's hand flew to her mouth when she realized that he had blood all over his shirt.

"Da! What happened?"

"It is not my blood. It's Abram's"

The color drained from Sadie's face, and she could barely speak above a whisper. "Where is he? Is he okay?"

"He's outside in the buggy. He cut his hand pretty badly, and I need you to drive him to the emergency room, while I go fetch John and Ruth."

"Of course." Sadie hurried out the door and ran across the yard toward Abram's buggy. She found Abram, pale-faced, cradling he left arm and holding a blood-soaked cloth around his hand. Sadie said a quick, silent prayer and looked at Abram. "How bad is it?"

Wincing in pain, Abram answered through gritted teeth. "It is pretty bad. I think I cut all the way to the bone."

"Oh no. Let me get your horse hitched up, and I'll get you right to the hospital. At least it isn't far."

"Thank you, Sadie."

Sadie quickly handled the horse and climbed into the buggy. "You do not need to thank me. I am happy to be able to help."

Sadie gently urged the horse forward, hoping to make the ride as comfortable as she could. Just before she pulled out onto the road, her father waved as he locked up the store.

Samuel looked anxious and called out to his daughter. "I'll get John and Ruth and meet you at the emergency room. Hurry, Sadie."

Once they were underway, traveling as quickly as Abram's horse could go, Sadie turned to Abram. "What happened?"

Holding his hand to his chest, Abram answered. "I was just careless. The chisel I was using slipped, and my left hand was in the way. I'm sure the chest I was working on will be stained and ruined."

"You know that is not what is important."

"I know. I just feel so stupid. I know better than to have made this mistake. I just hope there isn't permanent damage."

"Oh, Abram, I hadn't even thought about that."

"Let us not worry, Sadie. God will take care of me. Everything will be okay one way or another."

Sadie looked over at Abram, watching the way his jaw clenched because of the pain with every bump in the road. She had never worried about a person the way she worried for Abram now. She even found herself wondering what Abram would do for a living if he suffered permanent damage. How would he provide for his family? Urging the horse to move a little quicker, Sadie briefly closed her eyes and begged God to take care of Abram.

When they arrived at the hospital, Sadie wasn't exactly sure where she should park the buggy and tie up the horse. She pulled up to the emergency room entrance and helped Abram get out of the buggy, telling him to go inside and that she would join him when she had the horse taken care of. The ride hadn't been long, but she knew that if they stayed for any length of time, she would need both food and water for the horse. She hoped her father would be there by that time.

She found a place at the far edge of the parking lot where she could tie the horse up to a sign and park the buggy in an open parking space. Sadie had never been to a hospital before, and she was very conscious of the stares she received as she walked back toward the entrance. Sadie stifled a cough as she walked through the haze from the staff members congregated outside smoking cigarettes, and she was glad to be inside.

The inside of the hospital was a flurry of activity. Sadie looked around for Abram while she processed all of the strange equipment, smells, and people in the waiting room, none of whom looked happy. She finally saw him sitting down at a table speaking with a young woman who was simultaneously working at a computer and talking to Abram. Sadie threaded her way through all of the people and chairs to get to Abram. She put her hand on Abram's shoulder to let him know she was there while Abram explained that he didn't have medical insurance, but would be perfectly able to pay for his care.

The young woman finally looked up from the computer screen and looked at Sadie, examining every detail of her appearance, from the hand-stitched apron that Sadie wore, to the bonnet over her hair. The hospital employee looked at Abram.

"Is this your sister?"

Abram thought for a brief moment and answered. "No. She is my friend."

Sadie was looking around the room, taking in all of the people who were obviously waiting for care and she wondered how long Abram would have to wait.

The young woman stood up behind the desk. "If your hand is cut as badly as it sounds, we'll need to have you seen right away. Let me go find a nurse to take a look at you. Stay here. I'll be right back."

Relieved that Abram would be seen quickly, but worried that he might be seriously hurt, Sadie kept her hand on Abram's shoulder, realizing that she felt better in contact with his strong, broad shoulder.

"Are both of your parents home today?" Sadie asked Abram, trying to think of something to say rather than just standing there and worrying.

"I am not sure." Abram answered. "I am pretty sure Mother will be there, but I just do not know if Father had planned to run errands in town. He may have needed to deliver paperwork to some of his clients."

"I am sure Ruth will be worried. I hope Da gets here soon."

"Sadie, everything will be okay. I am glad you are here with me."

Sadie squeezed his shoulder and she saw the young woman coming back toward them.

"Come with me. We're super busy today, but I have a spot for you and a nurse ready to take a look."

Abram stood and Sadie moved to support him if

he needed help. They followed the woman down a hall, through double doors that required her to slide a card through a reader and into a room that held three beds, two of which were already occupied, curtains pulled partway closed to give some privacy. The woman gestured to the empty bed.

"Mary will be in shortly and she'll look you over to see if we need to get a doctor to you right away. Sit tight."

Abram sat on the edge of the bed and Sadie looked around the room.

"Want me to pull the curtain?" she asked.

"It does not matter to me," Abram answered as he tried to find a comfortable way to support his hand and keep it slightly elevated.

Sadie pulled the curtain around their section of the room while she listened to hear if she could figure out what was going on in the other two beds. Deciding that she should probably mind her own business, Sadie sat down in the chair next to Abram's bed. "Is there anything you need?"

"No. I am just trying to get comfortable. I hope this will not take too long." Abram paused to think. "If you want to leave, you can. You don't need to take care of me."

"Abram Byler, you cannot possibly think I would walk out and leave you here all alone and bleeding in a hospital," Sadie said indignantly. "What kind of person do you take me for?"

"That is not what I meant. I just meant…never mind. Forget I said it. I'm glad to have you here with me."

"That is better. I didn't have that much that I needed to get done at work today. I'm fine keeping you company."

Both Abram and Sadie looked up as the curtain was swept aside and a woman entered the space. She was short, wore bright pink scrubs, and her long silver hair was neatly pulled back into a low ponytail.

"My name's Mary. It's Abram, right?" she asked as she flipped through some paperwork.

Abram nodded and answered in the affirmative.

"Well, Abram, let me have a look at what's going on here." Mary stood at the edge of the bed and started to unwind the cloth that covered Abram's hand. The blood had dried and stiffened the fabric in the forty-five minutes since the accident, and Mary took care to remove it as gently as possible. "Oh my."

Sadie looked at Abram with a worried expression.

Mary folded the fabric back over the cut and took a step back. "Don't move. We have to get this stitched up right away."

Mary left the room, leaving the curtain wide open. Sadie stood and walked to Abram, even more anxious than before.

"Are you in a lot of pain?"

"It seems to be getting worse," Abram replied. "I was a little numb right after it happened, but that has worn off and it does hurt. I know I should probably hold it still, but I tried to move my thumb, and I don't think that I can. I am afraid that I did more than just cut myself."

"God will take care of you, Abram," Sadie said quietly. "I am sure of it."

Before Abram could say another word, Mary returned with a doctor in tow.

"Abram, this is Dr. Vasquez, and she's going to take care of you. She'll take a look, but I think we may need to move you to an operating room as soon as possible."

Dr. Vasquez smiled to Abram and Sadie and took a few steps toward the bed. "Mary tells me that you have a pretty deep cut, Abram. She's concerned that you may have damaged a tendon, too, so I need to take a look and determine how tough it's going to be to get you back together and good as new."

Dr. Vasquez uncovered Abram's hand, took one look and turned to Mary. "Get the O.R. ready. There's damage to one of the tendons. Can't tell how much, but we need to get in there and clean this up right away."

Sadie sat, wide-eyed and worried about Abram. Mary left the room and returned almost immediately with a wheelchair for Abram. As Abram sat down in the chair, Mary looked at Sadie. "I'll show you where you can wait after I get Abram into the O.R. He's going to be just fine. Dr. Vasquez is one of our best surgeons, and you're very lucky that she's on duty today."

Sadie followed Mary and Abram out into the hall, wishing that her father were with her. She knew that it would probably be at least another hour-and-a-half before Samuel returned with the Bylers, and Sadie decided that the best thing she could do for Abram was to stay calm and pray as if her life depended on it. Mary wheeled Abram into the operating room without another word, and Sadie realized that she wished she could have said something encouraging to Abram. Mary emerged from the room and put her arm around Sadie's shoulders.

"He'll be just fine, dear. Don't look so worried."

Mary walked Sadie to a small waiting room that wasn't currently occupied. Sadie looked around at the chairs, magazines and television and was grateful to have some privacy. Realizing that she was going to be at the hospital for a while, she turned to Mary.

"I know that this is going to be a strange question, but is there any way I can get some water for my horse?"

Mary's eyes widened. "Horse?"

"Yes. Horse. He's tied up in the parking lot, and he should be okay without food for a while, but I really need to get him some water."

Mary chuckled. "Of course. I'll have one of the maintenance crew run out and take care of it. I guess they won't have any trouble figuring out which horse is yours, right?"

Relieved at Mary's kind sense of humor and willingness to help, Sadie smiled back at the nurse. "Thank you so much for your help. How long will Abram be?"

"Oh I shouldn't imagine that he'll take any longer than a half hour or so. Even though the work is a little delicate, Dr. Vasquez is quick and very talented. He'll be out before you know it. He's a lucky man to have such a pretty girl in the waiting room for him." Mary headed out the door.

Sadie blushed. She was not at all used to receiving compliments on her appearance, and she was glad that none of her family and friends had heard Mary's comment. Sadie took a seat in one of the chairs and looked at the clock. She hoped that she wouldn't have long to wait before she could rejoin Abram. She said a prayer for God to guide the surgeon's hands, and she settled back and decided to take the rare opportunity to watch television.

The television was tuned to a morning talk show. Some statuesque blonde actress was talking about her wedding, and they showed photos from the big day. Sadie was fascinated and disgusted by all of the pearls, sparkles, makeup, and fabric in the pictures, and she couldn't understand why a person would spend so much time and money on a wedding that was more likely to end in divorce than not.

Watching the minutes pass on the clock that faced her, Sadie thought about how different her wedding day would be, compared to the blonde actress who talked about party favors and white doves. Sadie couldn't help but feel like the simpler ceremonies that her congregation held were much more meaningful than the huge celebrity weddings that ended up being shallow, self-indulgent displays focused on everything but a commitment to be together for life.

About forty minutes passed before Mary came back into the waiting room. Sadie stood up, anxious for news of Abram.

"He's doing great. He had almost completely severed a tendon, but Dr. Vasquez repaired it, stitched him up, and he should make a full recovery."

"Can I see him?"

"Of course. I'll take you to his room."

So pleased that Abram was through surgery, Sadie followed Mary through the hall to a private room. Abram lay in bed, covered with sheets, his hat on the bedside table.

"How are you feeling?"

"It hurts, but I am fine. The shot they gave me for the pain has almost completely worn off. Boy, I really did a number on my hand. Dr. Vasquez said that if I hadn't come in as quickly as I did, that I might not ever have regained full use of my hand."

Sadie moved to Abram's bedside and put her hand on his right arm. "Abram I was so worried for you. I thank God that you are going to be good as new."

As Sadie stood by Abram, she heard Mary's voice from the hallway outside the room.

"They're right in here, and he'll be just fine."

Abram and Sadie looked up as Samuel and Ruth came into the room. Ruth's eyes fell immediately on Sadie's hand on her son's arm, but Sadie was surprised to see no disapproval in her gaze. Sadie moved her hand and stepped out of the way to make room for Ruth to move to her son. While Ruth and Abram talked quietly, Sadie stood next to her father.

"I am so glad that you are here, Da. He did just fine, and the doctor said that he should make a full recovery. He very nearly cut all the way through his tendon, so he is lucky that they think they repaired it completely."

Samuel looked at Abram and Ruth. "I am surprised that the surgery was done this quickly."

"Mary, the nurse who brought you here, said that they had to get it done right away." Sadie was quiet for a moment. "Oh – did you see the horse in the parking lot? Did he have water?"

"Yes, we parked right next to you, and the horses are fine. How did you manage to get them water?"

"Mary had the maintenance man take care of it. She has been wonderful. Very kind."

Ruth turned to face Sadie and Samuel. "I cannot thank you enough for taking the time to get Abram to the hospital and come get me. He is lucky to work with people who care about him so much. If you need to go, I can stay with Abram now."

Samuel spoke. "Ruth, we will leave you and give you and Abram some privacy. I will come back by this evening to see if there is anything you need, and I will make sure Abram's horse is cared for. Samuel put his arm around Sadie and nodded to Abram.

"I will come back with Da, too," Sadie said before they left. "I am so glad that you will be okay."

Conscious of his mother's presence in the room, Abram thanked Sadie and hoped that his eyes could convey how much more he meant than he had been able to say. Ruth turned back to her son, and Sadie and Samuel left the room.

Samuel waited until he and Sadie were in the buggy heading back toward the workshop before he spoke. "I had a talk with Ruth on the way here. I won't say much since she wants to speak to you herself, but you will find that she has changed her mind about some things."

Sadie was stunned, staring at her father with her mouth hanging open. "Ruth? She wants to talk to me?" Sadie was used to Ruth avoiding her, refusing to make eye contact, and the prospect of Ruth wanting to have a conversation was hard for Sadie to fathom.

"I won't say any more about it, but I would ask you to hear her out. I think you will be surprised by what she has to say."

Knowing that her father would say nothing further, Sadie was left to wonder as they made the short drive back to the shop. What would Ruth Byler want to talk to her about? Uncomfortable at the prospect of having a conversation with Abram's mother, Sadie felt relieved when she realized that Ruth must want to talk to her about Jack Foster.

Sadie felt a little guilty about her disappointment when she realized that Ruth's concern was sure to be her health, rather than Sadie's relationship with Abram. Her dreams of Ruth's rescinding the ban on Abram and Sadie spending time together were likely just a fantasy, and Sadie reprimanded herself for even thinking about something so selfish when there were two people whose medical conditions were so much more important that Sadie's silly dreams.

Resolving to distract herself with work, Sadie started in on her list of things to do when they returned to the shop. Sadie worked quickly and efficiently, crossing one thing after another off the list, and before she knew it, the list was complete. Realizing that she still had some time, she sat down with her journal for a few minutes.

Having spent the morning with Abram had made her realize how much she had missed him, and how much she had enjoyed the times when they would share her journal – writing and responding to one another's entries. Though Sadie didn't really plan to share the journal with Abram again, she decided to indulge herself for a few minutes and write to him. Entry complete, the rest of the day flew by, and Samuel came into the store about an hour before they would typically stop working for the day.

"Sadie, are you in a position to close up? I thought we could go visit Abram and see if he and Ruth need anything."

Sadie looked around the store and decided that there was nothing urgent that needed her attention. "I can be ready in just a minute, Da. I'll lock up and meet you outside." Sadie picked up the lunch basket that she used each day, slipped her journal inside, turned out the lights, and locked the door, looking forward to seeing Abram.

Chapter Twenty-Four

When Sadie and Samuel arrived at the hospital, the first thing they did was take care of Abram's horse. It was clear that the maintenance team had kept the horse supplied with fresh water, and Samuel had thought to bring him some food. The horse seemed happy to see familiar faces and get something to eat.

The Zooks weren't sure if Abram would still be in the emergency room, or if he'd have been moved up to another room and kept overnight. They decided to try the E.R. first. They enquired at the front desk, and discovered that he was just about to be discharged, which they both took as a positive sign. They got directions to Abram's room – he'd been moved once again – and they set off to find him. Sadie put her hand over the pocket of her apron, feeling the outline of her little journal, safely concealed inside. She'd brought it just in case she had the opportunity to hand the book off to Abram. Though she wasn't sure, she thought there was a chance that he might be open to renewing the relationship they'd started months ago.

When they found Abram's room, Sadie looked around for Mary and was disappointed when she didn't see her. Just before they turned the corner to enter Abram's room, both Sadie and Samuel stopped short and looked at one another, puzzled and surprised to hear laughter coming from the room. Sadie rounded the corner first, and she could not have been more astonished at what she saw. Abram sat on the hospital bed, bandaged arm on his lap, looking at Ruth, seated in the chair in the tiny room. Ruth, in turn was smiling and listening to – of all people – Jack Foster!

"So I told her that no matter what my parents did to punish her, that I would still make her pay." Jack, Abram, and Ruth all dissolved in laughter, and Jack looked up as Sadie and Samuel entered the room. "Sadie! I was just telling Abram and Ruth about how unbearable my little sister was when we were growing up. It's a good thing she's reformed, or I wouldn't be here today."

Sadie couldn't say a word. She looked from person to person in the room and was just powerless to speak.

Samuel recovered from the surprise quicker than Sadie. "How is the hand, Abram?" he asked, opting for the obvious question. Samuel figured that whatever complex and improbable set of circumstances had put these three people all in the same room would be made clear in due course.

Abram looked down at his hand. "Not too bad. It still hurts, but Dr. Vasquez is pretty confident that I will be just fine. I have to see our regular doctor in a week so that he can take a look at it and decide when the stitches need to come out. She also said that I may need to go to physical therapy, but we will see."

Sadie stood still, mystified by the prospect of Ruth, Abram, and Jack all in the same room, laughing and talking as if it were perfectly normal. Not sure what to say, Sadie shook her head as if to wake herself up, discovered that the scene in the room was still the same, fixed Abram with a questioning look, and waited for someone to explain.

Jack stood up from his seat at the corner of Abram's bed. "Here, Sadie, have a seat. I should probably get going anyway. I suspect that my sister's tests are finished and she'll be ready to go."

Sadie looked at Jack and finally found her voice. "How did you? What are you doing here?"

Jack laughed and answered. "Oh that? Just a convenient coincidence, really. I brought my sister here to the lab to have a few tests run before we start her treatment next week. I came down to the E.R. to chat with a few folks – I did my residence here – and I saw Abram. We got to talking and now I should probably go find my sister."

Jack took a couple of steps toward the doorway and looked at Ruth. "It was nice to meet you, and I look forward to seeing you and meeting your husband next week. Abram, you take care of yourself – no more playing with sharp objects, you hear?"

Sadie sat down heavily on the edge of the bed. She realized right away that she was witnessing a miracle of sorts. There was only one way to explain what had just happened and that was that God had taken control.

Ruth smiled at Jack. "It was nice to meet you too, and I thank you for taking the time to meet with us. You are very kind."

Abram realized why Sadie was so stunned, and in fact he was surprised, too, at how easily Jack had charmed his mother, a no nonsense woman who typically forbid idle talk as the tool of the Devil. Abram had been worried that Ruth's dour countenance would make Jack wish he hadn't offered to meet with Ruth, but Jack didn't even seem to notice, and in no time, the doctor had put her at ease.

Abram looked at Sadie. "This may sound strange, but I am worried for my horse. Is he okay?"

"Yes. Da brought him some feed, and they kept him supplied with fresh water while we were gone. He is just fine." Sadie looked at Ruth and then Abram again. "So everything is okay?"

"It is. I am free to go." Abram looked at his mother. "I am so glad that you got to meet Dr. Foster and get to know him a little."

"I am as well. I believe that God has led us to this point, and I feel certain that going to see Dr. Foster is the right thing to do."

Sadie was relieved and pleased all at once that Ruth had agreed to meet with Jack and that she also didn't seem to be upset with Sadie. It had been quite a day, and Sadie realized how tired she was as she stifled a yawn. Nothing wore her out like emotional events. To have been so worried for Abram and to have been anticipating the conversation that Ruth wanted to have with her had just about done Sadie in.

Abram stood up. "I am ready to be out of this place. Mother, are you ready to leave?"

Ruth stood as well. "I am. You and Samuel go ahead. I want to talk to Sadie for a minute."

Sadie felt a little panicked as Abram and Samuel left the room. She took a deep breath and hoped that what Ruth had to say wouldn't be unpleasant.

"Sadie, I want to thank you, both for taking care of Abram and getting him here safely and quickly, but also for introducing Abram to Dr. Foster. That was an unselfish and humble thing to do. There is more that I would like to say to you, but I know that today is not the right time. Would you consider coming over for coffee tomorrow evening? Abram can drive you home afterwards if he feels up to it."

Sadie looked at Ruth and wondered if the day's surprises would ever end. "I would be happy to join you for coffee," she answered simply.

"Good. I will see you then." Ruth walked out of the room and Sadie stood and hurried after her.

When Sadie and Ruth emerged from the hospital, it was getting close to dinnertime, and Sadie realized that in addition to being tired, she was also hungry. She hoped that her mother wouldn't worry that they would be home a little later than usual. It was strange to see Abram sitting in the buggy, waiting for his mother to climb up and take the reins, but clearly the best thing for his injured hand was rest.

As the Zooks and the Bylers parted ways until the morning, Sadie remembered the little journal in her pocket. Since Ruth was sitting right next to Abram, though, Sadie decided to hold on to the book. Maybe, if tomorrow's coffee meeting went well, Sadie might hope to be able to begin sharing her journal with Abram without having to hide it.

Samuel realized that Sadie was a little shaken by the day's events. He knew that it had been hard for her to end the relationship that she and Abram had begun in June, and it couldn't have been easy to spend so much of the day so close to him. He also knew that Sadie had to feel anxious about talking to Ruth, and he knew that what Ruth had to say to Sadie would take far longer than the brief moments they had shared in the hospital.

"Everything okay?" Samuel asked Sadie as they started the trip home.

"I do not know. I am almost afraid to hope that things will work out the way I would like them to. I know that I need to just put my faith in God and know that everything will happen according to His plan. Sadie paused for a moment. "I am embarrassed to admit that I am a little afraid of Ruth. She invited me for coffee tomorrow evening. I know that she has accused me of behaving improperly in the past, and I have trouble believing that having coffee with her will be anything other than unpleasant. Is that a horrible thing to say, Da?"

Samuel smiled at his daughter. He had to try hard not to be proud of her and amused by her all at the same time. "Sadie, you know I have spoken with Ruth, and you can trust me that everything will be fine. She has said unkind things about you in the past, but I would urge you to follow the example of the Lord and find it in your heart to forgive her. Every person is a sinner, and every one of us requires forgiveness."

Sadie thought about her father's wise words, and she decided that one of the things she would pray for this evening was the humility to look past her hurt feelings and the willingness to hear Ruth with an open mind.

As Samuel guided the horse into the Zook's yard, the sun was beginning to set, and Sadie could see her family seated inside at the dinner table. Looking inside through the dining room windows, Sadie found that she looked forward to going inside to share a meal and spending the evening with her warm, loving family. She was glad to see that they hadn't held dinner to wait for the latecomers.

Sadie headed inside first, as Samuel stayed in the barn to feed and water the horse. She hurried to the door, pulled both by her empty stomach and by the worry that she knew would be troubling her mother.

"We're home," Sadie called as she walked through the door.

"Where have you been?" Hannah asked as she filled plates for Samuel and Sadie. "I knew that if something awful had happened that you would have called the Kobels to let us know, but I was still worried."

Sadie sat at the table and shared the news of the day's events with her family between bites. She was certain that the crisp edges of her mother's sweet cornbread and fresh butter had never tasted better than they did that evening.

It wasn't often that she was late for a meal, and as she spooned her first bite of ham, slow cooked with green beans and black-eyed peas, Sadie savored the flavor of the food and her pleasure at being home with her family.

Her family was worried about Abram, relieved at his prognosis, and they were all surprised and pleased to hear that Ruth had agreed to see Dr. Foster. Sadie didn't bring up the topic of having coffee with Ruth the next day, deciding that she'd talked enough and was ready for bed despite the early hour. Sadie helped her mother and sisters clean up and headed upstairs to wash her face and go to bed.

Finally in bed, Sadie said her prayers and asked God for guidance and patience in her dealings with Ruth the next day. It hadn't been that long ago that Ruth and John Byler had stood in her parents' parlor and said awful, untrue things about Sadie. Knowing that God would want her to forgive any wrongs, Sadie prayed that she would be able to do that and listen to Ruth with an open mind.

As tired as she was, Sadie didn't sleep well. She kept waking from awful dreams – she dreamed that Abram had been killed while working with razor sharp tools. She dreamed that her parents had believed Ruth and John and had thrown her out of the house and shunned her for the rest of her life. She also dreamed of having coffee with Ruth, and in the dream, Ruth was horrid to Sadie – locking her in the cellar for weeks at a time, only letting her out to wash dishes and prepare meals. Worst of all, in her dream about Ruth, Abram's mother had absolutely prohibited Abram from ever speaking to Sadie again, regardless of the circumstances. Sadie finally woke just before dawn, feeling hollow and apprehensive. She could only hope that her day would improve.

As she worked in the kitchen combining spicy sausage, fresh spinach, day-old bread, scrambled eggs, and grated cheddar cheese for a breakfast casserole, Sadie realized that she might not even see Abram at work today. With his injured hand, she wasn't sure that he'd be able to get any work done, and he might even have trouble handling the horse on the way to work. She supposed that she'd find out when she got there. With a few minutes to spare before she needed to meet her father outside for their drive to the shop, Sadie asked Miriam if they could speak privately for a minute or two.

Miriam sat down at the kitchen table with another cup of coffee. "Is something wrong?"

"Not exactly. I just have a couple of questions for you since you have much more experience with courting than I do."

Miriam smiled knowingly at Sadie. "Ah. So have you finally found a replacement for Abram, then?"

Sadie sat down with her sister. "No, that is part of the problem. I have not found anyone else, and this whole situation – with Dr. Foster and Ruth – has meant that I've spent a lot more time talking to Abram over the last couple of days. I also spent most of the morning with him at the hospital, and Miriam, nothing has changed between us. He is still the most interesting and best man I've talked to as a potential suitor."

"So what is the problem, then?"

"You know the history. How Ruth and John made Abram stop courting me and how they talked to Da and Mama and said things about me that were not true. "

Miriam reached out and squeezed Sadie's hand. "I remember."

"So I was really surprised yesterday when Ruth not only agreed to see Dr. Foster, but was also pleasant to me. She hasn't made eye contact with me in months, but she invited me to come over for coffee after work today. She wants to talk to me."

"Wow. That is quite a change, isn't it?" Miriam thought for a moment. "I do not know what to say. I have never had any troubles with Luke's mother. She pretends not to know that we are courting, though that will change soon."

Sadie got excited. "Really? Is there to be an announcement soon?"

Practically everyone knew that Miriam and Luke Stoltzfos would be married in the fall, and it was getting close to the time of year when the couples who planned to wed in the fall would make their announcements.

Miriam beamed as she answered. "We're going to announce it at the next church service, and we will be getting married at the beginning of November."

"I am so happy for you."

"Thank you, Sadie. To get back to your situation, though, I think that your best course of action is to approach the meeting with a hopeful, humble heart and to be certain that God's will always prevails. Trust in the Lord and he will guide your steps."

Sadie smiled at her sister. "Thank you. I am sure that you are right, but I can't help being a little anxious. I will be so happy when I know what is on Ruth's mind. Whether it is good or bad, I will be happier when I no longer have to wonder." Sadie peeked out the window and saw Samuel at the buggy. "I have to run. I will see you this evening."

Miriam sat at the table for a few moments longer. She hoped that her sister would find happiness – if not with Abram, then with another good man. Miriam also thought about how lucky she was that Luke had such a sweet mother. Miriam was quite sure that Ruth Byler wouldn't be her first choice as a potential mother-in law. Remembering that she'd promised Hannah that she would wash the outsides of all of the windows in the house, Miriam realized that she was going to have a busy day. Hoping that her work would keep her busy until Sadie got home, Miriam rolled up her sleeves, got her rags and a bucket full of vinegar and water, and headed outside to find the ladder.

Arriving at work, Sadie wasn't entirely surprised that Abram's little courting buggy wasn't at the shop already. She imagined that he'd woken up sore, assuming that he'd managed to get any sleep at all. Sadie and Samuel parted ways and began their work. It wasn't long before Sadie looked out the window and saw John Byler pull into the yard. He climbed down from the wagon and Sadie dashed outside, anxious for some news of Abram.

"John. Good morning," Sadie called. "How is Abram feeling this morning?"

"Oh, he will be fine, Lord willing. He was very sore this morning, and he said he slept poorly. I doubt he would be much use to Samuel today, so he's going to come in this afternoon if he feels much better."

Sadie was a little disappointed that she may not see Abram, because if he didn't come in to work, then she'd have no way to get to see Ruth that evening. She supposed that the talk would just have to wait another day or two.

"Oh, I forgot, Sadie. Ruth asked me to tell you that if Abram doesn't come in to work, she'll have Joshua or John come fetch you for coffee."

Not quite sure if she should be relieved or more anxious, Sadie assured John that either arrangement would be fine, and she headed back inside to finish working on creating the advertisement that she'd convinced her father to run in the Christmas flyer that advertised local businesses in collaboration with the Chamber of Commerce. She was hoping that the ad would be successful in bringing them some higher dollar business so that they could focus their time more efficiently.

As Sadie got back to work on proofreading her text, she was distracted by her delight that she would get to see Abram this evening one way or another. She hoped that he would come pick her up, as that would allow her some time with him privately, but she'd settle for just seeing him face to face and seeing first hand how he was feeling.

After lunch, Sadie walked into town to buy some stamps and a few other office supplies. She also mailed the Christmas ad so that it would arrive on time. It only had to go across town, but it was more convenient to mail it than to borrow the buggy for the trip across some of Ephrata's busiest roads. Sadie was deep in thought, contemplating the other ads she might run if this first one was a success when a car horn honked right next to her, scaring her out of her skin.

Turning to give the driver a dirty look – which would be as far as Sadie dared go in expressing her displeasure, she saw her friend Meredith, in her sports car, top down, hair in a ponytail, and sunglasses on. Meredith pulled to the side of Main Street and the girls chatted briefly. They were about to part ways when Sadie realized that she hadn't told Meredith about Abram's accident the day before.

Meredith looked horrified and finally relieved when Sadie got to the end of the story and shared his prognosis. "Well if he needs anything, just let me know. Mom can fit him in at her office if necessary. I'm sure his doctor is fine, but if there's any problem at all, let me know. I can even pick him up if he needs a ride."

Sadie was touched by the unexpected gift she'd been given in this sweet, thoughtful, and completely atypical friend that she'd made a few months ago. "Thank you, Meredith. That means a lot to me, and I will be sure to tell Abram."

Meredith offered Sadie a lift to the post office, but Sadie declined, actually enjoying her walk in the lovely, early autumn sunshine. Errands complete, Sadie walked back to work and was delighted to see Abram's buggy in the yard. Expecting to find Abram in the workshop, Sadie hurried inside, only to find her father there alone.

Before Sadie could even say a word, Samuel spoke up. "He is not here. He probably should not even have driven, so I sent him over to the store to sit down. Don't you put him to work, Sadie Zook."

Shaking her head at her father's crazy thought that she would even dream of doing such a thing, Sadie headed back toward the store. Excited to see Abram, but concerned at her father's evaluation of his condition, Sadie opened the door to find Abram stretched out on a daybed along the wall, sound asleep. Tiptoeing over to the bed, Sadie relished the chance to look at Abram unobserved. She noticed the crease from his hat in his brown hair, his long eyelashes, and his strong, work-hardened hands – well one hand, anyway. His left hand was wrapped in gauze and rested on a pillow to keep it slightly elevated.

While Sadie stood over him, Abram shifted and opened his eyes. Had Sadie been able to read his mind, she would have blushed for sure, and may have even walked out of the room angry. Abram couldn't really help it though, that the first thought he'd had was that Sadie's face was one that he thought he could wake up to for the rest of his life. He started to sit up, and Sadie stopped him with a hand on his uninjured arm.

"No need to sit up, Abram," Sadie told him quietly. "You can lie still and rest while I finish up my work."

Chapter Twenty-Five

The drive to the Byler's house was a little strange. Abram was clearly in pain, and Sadie was worried about his being jostled in the buggy, but there wasn't much she could do about it. She desperately wanted to know what the topic of Ruth's conversation would be, and she suspected that Abram knew, but he'd completely deflected all of her attempts to get him to talk about it. She supposed that she would have to wait and find out on her own.

Deciding to just enjoy the time alone with Abram, Sadie thought that it might be fun to see if she could get a little rise out of him. "So I was talking to Miriam this morning. Do not tell anyone, but she and Luke are going to announce their plans to marry at the next church service."

Abram looked over at Sadie. "That is wonderful. I will congratulate both of them as soon as they make it public."

"Yes. Miriam was telling me that I ought to start thinking about settling down, too. She knew that I was fond of you, but since you threw me over, she suggested that perhaps I think about Stephen Sommer. What do you think? I mean he is tall like you. I suppose that's a good start…" Sadie trailed off as if she were deep in thought considering her options for another suitor. She peeked at Abram from the corner of her eye.

Abram started to reply and caught a glimpse of Sadie's partially concealed grin. He realized that she was just trying to get a reaction from him, and so he said something that he hoped she wasn't expecting. "Yes, Stephen Sommer would be an excellent choice. My father has started doing the books for his father's farm. Would you like me to have Father say something?"

Sadie was startled, surprised that Abram had played along with her teasing. She looked at him and laughed. "Why, Abram Byler, did you just make a joke?"

"Did not think I had it in me, did you?" Abram asked, a bit smug.

Sadie looked at him, more serious now. "A little surprise every now and then isn't all bad."

"No, I suppose you are right, Sadie. I am surprised, for example, to be sitting in the buggy with you on our way for you to have a visit with my mother, that is for sure."

"That makes two of us, Abram."

Sadie was nervous as they pulled into the Bylers' yard. Glad to see Sarah outside taking clothes off the line, Sadie waved at her before she climbed down and had to stop Abram from attempting to unhitch his horse.

"Let Joshua or John do it. You should rest that hand."

Abram discovered that he didn't really mind Sadie fussing over him a bit, and he used his good right arm to guide her toward the kitchen door. They crossed the yard, and he opened the door for her. Ruth and Katie were in the kitchen, hard at work making little potato dumplings for dinner.

Ruth looked up from her work and smiled at Abram and Sadie. "I will be finished here shortly. Abram go ahead and take Sadie into the parlor and I'll put some coffee on." Ruth looked at Katie and winked. "Unless you would rather help your sister make dumplings?"

Abram and Sadie looked at one another as if they'd seen a three-headed cat. Ruth Byler just winked and made a joke? Was the world coming to an end? Abram shrugged his shoulders and took Sadie into the next room. He directed her to the most comfortable chair in the room, a rocking chair that had been his maternal grandmother's, and Sadie had a seat. It was only a few minutes before Ruth joined them.

Ruth settled in her rocking chair. "Coffee will be ready shortly. Sadie, I have already spoken with Abram, so I am going to ask him to give us some privacy."

"Okay," was all that Sadie could think of to say.

After Abram left the room, Ruth looked at Sadie and began. "To start with, Sadie, I owe you an apology. Now some of what I have to say to you will be hard for me to say, and if you do not mind, I would like to ask you to just let me finish. It will be easier that way. Is that okay?"

Sadie nodded her assent.

"First of all, I owe you an apology. I judged you unfairly. When I found your journal, all I could see was a flighty young girl ready to be seduced by the world. The reason that I had such a strong reaction to your journal is that I could see myself – thirty years ago – in you. I did not want that sort of girl for my son. It worried me that Abram clearly had feelings for you, and I thought you would ruin his life. I now think that I was wrong."

Ruth shifted in her chair and continued. "Having been sick has forced me to think about things that I have been trying my whole life to forget – mistakes I made that have made me who I am. I felt like I deserved to be punished, to be unhappy because I made some mistakes when I was about your age. Those mistakes have haunted me, made me afraid of the bad choices that my children could make, and made me profoundly unhappy because at one point in my life, my faith wavered. I have lived my entire adult life believing that being Plain and being humble meant being unhappy. I was wrong.

"When I was diagnosed with cancer, I thought that it must have been punishment from God. I prayed and prayed that God forgive me for my youthful transgressions, and one night – one of the many nights that I would sit in this very chair, unable to sleep – one night, while the whole house was quiet, I realized that God had forgiven me. Forgiven me long ago. The problem was that I had not forgiven myself. I had wasted all these years being unhappy because I believed that I didn't deserve to be happy."

Ruth stood up. "I'm sure the coffee is ready. Would you like some cream?"

Sadie sat back in her chair, stunned by what Ruth had said so far. "No thank you. Black is fine."

Ruth came back in the room with two cups of coffee, and she handed one to Sadie. "I will not go into details about the mistakes that I made as a girl, but I will tell you that I risked my community and my faith for what ended up being a shallow and meaningless relationship. I stopped short of making decisions that would be irreversible, but I did consider leaving our community. I am ashamed to admit that, but it is important to face our flaws.

"Sadie, I want Abram to make good decisions, and I want him to learn to trust the Lord to guide his steps. When John and I told Abram that he could no longer court you, I thought that I was doing the right thing. I realize now that I was probably wrong."

Sadie was overwhelmed by Ruth's revelations. She stood up and walked to the window, looking out into the pumpkin field next to the house. Hoping that Ruth would give her a moment to absorb everything, Sadie stared out the window and dared to hope that Ruth was about to share the best news possible. Sadie turned back to face Ruth, walked to her chair, and sat down again.

Ruth continued. "Sadie, when Abram told me that you had been involved in setting up the introduction to Dr. Foster, I knew right away that God had used your presence in my life to teach me a lesson. That you – a girl I'd berated and labeled worldly – would be the one to see the Hand of God at work in our lives and unselfishly see to it that Abram met Dr. Foster…that just confirmed the lessons that I had been learning throughout this ordeal.

"I will not stand in the way of Abram courting you, Sadie. In fact, I believe that you may well be the very person that God has in mind for Abram. You seem to understand him, and I think that you will be good for him."

Sadie finally spoke. "Does Abram know all of this?"

"Yes. I have spoken with him, and I asked that he let me talk to you myself. I am so sorry, Sadie. I have wronged you, and I hope that both you and the Lord will forgive me."

As the realization that she was free to see Abram again finally began to occur to Sadie, she grinned. "Of course, Ruth. This is just a lot to take in all at once."

"I am sure it is, and I need to go check on dinner, so I will give you a little time to yourself. Will you stay for dinner?"

Sadie thought about it and figured that her parents wouldn't mind if she came home just a little late. "Thank you. I would love to stay, but I will need to leave right afterwards so that my parents do not worry."

"I will have Sarah set another place."

Sadie sat in the rocking chair, hardly able to believe what had just happened. She knew that Ruth's change of heart must have truly been the work of God, and she was astonished that even out of something as difficult as cancer, the Lord could find a way to teach beautiful lessons.

Abram walked into the parlor, as happy as Sadie had

ever seen him. He sat next to Sadie and looked at her, noticing that she had tears shining in her eyes. "You are crying? What is wrong?"

"Oh, Abram, nothing is wrong. I am just so overwhelmed. Your mother was kind and wonderful, and we can see one another again. It is just all so sudden and surprising."

The dinner bell rang outside, interrupting the sweet conversation between Abram and Sadie, and they walked into the dining room together. Sadie's place was set right next to Abram's, and Sadie hadn't realized how hungry she was until the aroma of potato dumplings in sauce with a hint of nutmeg reached her. Dinner was delicious, and while conversation wasn't quite as brisk as it would have been at the Zook's house, Ruth did share the news with everyone that she would be meeting with Dr. Foster next week and was hopeful that he would be able to treat her.

They Bylers looked relieved, as they knew that Ruth had wrestled with her decision and had spent hours in prayer. Sadie was surprised when Ruth made a point of letting everyone know that it was Sadie who had discovered that Dr. Foster was an oncologist, and it was Sadie who had arranged the meeting.

"I know that God would not have hurt Abram's hand, but I cannot help but think that it was somehow part of His plan that I was in the hospital yesterday. Dr. Foster put me right at ease, and I truly believe that it is God's will that I go see him. I know that the Lord will work everything out." Ruth's statement was made with a calm, warm certainty that Sadie and the rest of the Bylers found new and heartwarming.

Sadie offered to help clear and clean up dinner, but Ruth shooed her out of the kitchen and reminded her that she needed to get home so that her parents wouldn't worry. Sadie thanked Ruth, both for the meal and for the conversation, and Sadie headed outside to find Abram.

As Sadie looked at Abram, tall and strong as he hitched the horse to his buggy, Sadie realized how very lucky she was. Not only had she rediscovered the wonderful connection with Abram, but now she had the blessing of his parents. Knowing that Ruth approved of her made all the difference to Sadie.

Abram turned from his work to see Sadie watching him. He swept his arm toward his buggy in a grand gesture of invitation. "Your chariot, ma'am."

Sadie giggled and extended her hand for Abram to help her into the buggy. "Why thank you, sir," she replied formally.

As Abram climbed into the buggy, Sadie saw him wince in pain.

"Are you sure you are up to the drive?" she asked in concern. "I am sure that one of your brothers will drive me home if you need to rest."

"Sadie, nothing could keep me from driving you home this evening. I have been looking forward to this drive all day." Abram paused and thought. "Actually, I have been looking forward to this drive for much longer than that, but I was not sure it would ever happen." They pulled out of the yard in companionable silence and rode for a few hundred yards.

Abram was the first to speak. "Sadie, you were right, you know. I should have trusted that God would work everything out. I just never realized that being happy – the way I felt with you – might be a sign from God that I was on the right path. It took you to teach me that lesson."

Abram looked over at the young woman beside him in the buggy. While he knew that no human could be perfect, Abram thought that she might just be perfect for him. He wanted to reach out and take her hand, but he needed his one good hand to hold the reins. Sadie saw him trying to figure out the logistics – seeing if there were a way that he could touch her and still drive the buggy.

Stifling a laugh, Sadie slid over a little closer and leaned over to be right next to Abram. She was both comforted and thrilled by the heat of his hip next to hers, and being close to him felt perfectly right. She sighed happily, worn out from another emotionally draining day, but so hopeful and positive that her future with Abram was a bright one, blessed by the Lord.

Pleased to have Sadie at his side, Abram looked down at her, falling into the pools of her blue eyes. "So, Sadie, will you allow me to come call on you this Sunday since we do not have church? Maybe we could go get some ice cream in town?"

"I cannot think of anything I would like better."

"And can I drive you home from church the next Sunday?"

"Of course."

"And what about the church service after that?"

"Absolutely. As many as you would like."

The young couple snuggled and talked on the drive that didn't last nearly as long as they would have liked, and Abram reluctantly turned into the Zook's drive. He pulled on the reins and stopped the horse, and Sadie refused to let him descend to help her out. Giving him strict instructions to take care of his hand, she climbed down and reached into the pocket of her apron.

"Abram, I wrote something for you, and I wonder if you would consider resuming our writing to one another?" Sadie held out her oldest journal – the green fabric covered one that Abram had first found months ago. "You do not have to answer, but I would like for you to read it."

Abram accepted the journal with a laugh. "What a coincidence. I bought a journal a few days ago thinking that it might help me make sense of the things that I was struggling with. After Mother told me last night that she would let me court you, I stayed up a few extra minutes to write an entry for you as well." Abram reached under his seat, pulled out a blue journal, and handed it to Sadie.

Abram and Sadie looked at one another, full of the wonder and promise that the day had given them. Secure in the knowledge that it was God's will that they be together, their parting that evening was sweet and brief, for they knew that this was just the beginning of the relationship that would last them the rest of their days.

Epilogue

Two years later

Abram left work, bidding goodbye to Samuel Zook and packing up his lunch pail. He found that he missed the days when Sadie used to pack a lunch for all three of them. Since Sadie had stopped working at Ephrata Woodworks, though, Samuel hadn't found the right person to replace her. Sadie's friend Meredith stopped in two mornings a week to handle phone calls and make sense of the paperwork that had accumulated in her absence, but Samuel knew that it was just a matter of time before God put the right person in place.

Abram whistled as he hitched up his horse to his buggy. He seldom used his little two-seater buggy any longer, and he was considering selling it to his youngest brother, John, now seventeen. Happy to be heading home, Abram wondered if Sadie would have found enough time to prepare their dinner. She'd had her hands full of late, with her household duties and the added work of helping his mother get ready for Joshua Byler's wedding dinner.

Arriving at home, Abram felt the deep satisfaction that he experienced every day when he returned home to the woman he both loved and respected. He took care of the horse, tossed some feed into the chicken coop, and decided to check in on Sadie before he started on the rest of his chores.

As soon as Abram entered the kitchen, he smelled herbs and roast chicken and saw his favorite recipe of Sadie's – her cinnamon bread – cooling on the counter. Surprised that the kitchen was quiet and empty, Abram walked through into the sitting room and paused in the doorway to savor the scene before him. Sadie sat in her rocking chair, golden hair lit by the lamp next to her, writing in her journal. Her foot was extended to periodically rock the cradle in front of her and keep the precious little girl inside fast asleep.

Sadie looked up as Abram approached and gave first Sadie, then little Ruth, a kiss on the forehead.

"How are my girls," he asked softly.

"Good. Ruth's been asleep for nearly an hour, and I thought I'd take advantage of the quiet to do a little writing."

Abram looked down at the slim pink volume, a journal he'd not seen before. "What are you writing now?" he asked.

"It is for Ruth. I decided to record my thoughts and feelings to share with her one day."

Abram smiled at the woman who had become so

dear to him. "I am sure she will enjoy it as much as I have enjoyed your journals for me. I must go start the chores." Abram left the room, happy and grateful to God for the gifts in his life.

Sadie watched him leave, opened her journal again, and began to write.

Email Newsletter

Sign up for email alerts. Your email address will never be given away and you can unsubscribe at any time.

http://eepurl.com/AY3J9

CPSIA information can be obtained at www.ICGtesting.com
Printed in the USA
LVOW10s1716080913

351505LV00018B/294/P